LIGHT IN THE DARKNESS

A Stage Adaptation Inspired by
Victor Hugo's Les Misérables

Heather Neumann

Edition 2
First printing, 2025

ISBN 979-8-9933358-1-0

PLEASE NOTE…
Producing *Light in the Darkness* is both an exciting and
meaningful endeavor, and we ask that all groups honor the
work by securing the proper performance rights. As with any
published play, royalties are required for each performance.
Royalties not only ensure that the author is compensated for
their creative labor but also help sustain future projects and
adaptations.
Whether you are a school, community theater, or church
group, please reach out for licensing information before
staging your production. Securing these rights is simple and
ensures your cast and audience can enjoy the story with
integrity and excellence. We are thrilled to see *Light in the
Darkness* brought to life in new communities and look
forward to partnering with you as you share this powerful
story on stage. Please contact heather@lastingimpact.info

CONTENTS

AUTHOR'S NOTE

Les Misérables by Victor Hugo, first published in 1862, is widely considered one of the greatest novels of the 19th century. This adaptation of *Les Misérables* seeks to honor the emotional depth and spiritual power of Victor Hugo's novel while presenting it in a clear, poetic, and performable format for the stage. At its heart, this is a story of grace and transformation, of justice and mercy, of suffering and hope. The scenes move swiftly—yet the human drama remains constant, within the theme of light and dark. Every character, from the noblest to the most fallen, is wrestling with who they are and what they believe in a world both beautiful and broken. This version embraces the novel's moral weight and emotional grandeur while offering room for creativity, intimacy, and simplicity in staging.

Though the story spans decades and revolutions, it is ultimately about a single soul's journey toward redemption—and the people he changes along the way. The tone of this piece is reverent, lyrical, and urgent. It leans into the contrasts of high and low, laughter and lament, law and love. While the language is elevated, it is meant to be spoken with clarity and feeling (often in Hugo's own words). Directors and performers are encouraged to approach the script not as a museum piece, but as a living story with modern resonance. Play it with honesty. Carry its truth gently. And let its grace move you.

With Warm Regards,

Heather Neumann

CHARACTER DESCRIPTIONS

There are roles for well over 40 actors in this production. Some roles can be double cast. There is flexibility in casting.

Jean Valjean (200+ lines)

Jean Valjean is the moral and emotional center of Les Misérables. A former convict imprisoned for stealing bread, Valjean is transformed by an act of mercy and spends the rest of his life seeking redemption. On stage, he must be portrayed with gravitas, compassion, and quiet strength. The actor should reflect both the torment of his past and the nobility of his renewed purpose. His journey is one of internal transformation—his struggle to live righteously under the burden of his past gives the story its soul. The performance should show his deep empathy, especially in his relationships with Fantine, Cosette, and Marius, and his stoic dignity even in suffering.

Javert (90+ lines)

Javert is a police inspector obsessed with order, law, and justice—believing them to be one and the same. Born in a prison and rising through the ranks by sheer discipline, he lives by an unyielding moral code where the law is absolute and inflexible. On stage, Javert must be portrayed with a commanding presence, internal rigidity, and a deep sense of moral duty. He is not a villain in the traditional sense; he is sincere, but tragically misguided. His downfall comes when he is confronted by Valjean's mercy, which shatters his black-and-white worldview. The role requires intensity and stoicism, but also a gradual, silent unraveling—culminating in his final moment of existential collapse.

Fantine (70+ lines)

Fantine is a symbol of innocence betrayed and a society's failure to protect its most vulnerable. A young working-class woman abandoned by her lover and forced into desperation to care for her child, she is eventually ruined by poverty, injustice, and shame. On stage, Fantine must be portrayed with a raw, emotional vulnerability that captures both her early hope and her later despair. She is gentle but strong-willed, clinging to love for her daughter as her only purpose. The actor should allow Fantine's decline to feel inevitable yet tragic, a quiet indictment of the world around her. Her presence lingers beyond her death, sanctifying Valjean's journey and Cosette's legacy.

Cosette (40+ lines)

Cosette begins as a neglected and abused child, but through Valjean's care she becomes a symbol of purity, hope, and renewal. In the novel, she is described as beautiful, sheltered, and kind, somewhat idealized but not without agency. On stage, Cosette should be played with quiet strength, warmth, and a tender heart. She is not naïve—her sheltered life creates longing, curiosity, and a deep capacity for love. Her romance with Marius should feel sincere and sweet, a contrast to the world's harshness. While she may appear secondary, Cosette represents the life Valjean sacrifices everything to protect. Her transformation from frightened child to confident young woman mirrors his redemption.

Marius (50+ lines)

Marius Pontmercy is a young man caught between heritage, idealism, and love. Raised by his royalist grandfather but secretly admiring his republican father, he is torn by generational loyalties and social expectations. In the novel, he is intelligent, romantic, and introspective—often lost in thought, literature, or political passion. On stage, Marius must balance youthful fervor with emotional vulnerability. He should be played with sincerity and a touch of awkward charm, especially in his infatuation with Cosette. His journey is one of maturation—learning to suffer, to choose, and ultimately, to love with selflessness. He is not a revolutionary leader, but a man changed by revolution.

Éponine (30+ lines)

Éponine, once a spoiled child, grows into a streetwise teenager hardened by neglect, poverty, and unrequited love. Yet beneath the grime and sarcasm lies a tender, fiercely loyal soul. On stage, Éponine must be played with grit and yearning. She is scrappy and bold, navigating a harsh world with defiance and dark humor, but her moments of quiet longing—especially toward Marius—must feel raw and real. Her love is selfless and sacrificial, culminating in her death to save the one she loves. She represents the overlooked, the unwanted, and the redemptive power of choosing love anyway.

Azelma (20+ lines)

Azelma is the younger daughter of the Thénardiers and serves as a quiet contrast to her sister Éponine. In Victor Hugo's novel, she is obedient, impressionable, and remains loyal to her parents' schemes without question. Unlike Éponine, who develops a moral conscience, Azelma stays entangled in her family's corruption, representing the tragedy of a child shaped entirely by her environment. On stage, she should be played as watchful, submissive, and eager to please—perhaps a bit jealous of Éponine's strength—bringing subtlety and realism to the Thénardiers' chaotic world.

Gavroche (20+ lines)

Gavroche is the embodiment of Parisian Street life—cheeky, brave, clever, and full of fight. He is the son of the Thénardiers, though he disowns them, making his own way in the world with swagger and songs. In the novel, Gavroche is a symbol of youthful rebellion and irrepressible spirit. On stage, he should be portrayed with energetic charm and sharp wit—confident, mischievous, and surprisingly wise. He's a child of the barricades, fearless in the face of bullets and injustice. Though he provides comic relief, his death is one of the story's most poignant moments. Gavroche reminds the audience that courage doesn't require size, and innocence can still burn bright in war.

Enjolras (20+ lines)

Enjolras is the passionate leader of the student revolutionaries—the Friends of the ABC. He is the embodiment of youthful idealism and fierce dedication to republican justice. In the novel, he is described as angelically beautiful, austere, and almost otherworldly in his conviction. On stage, Enjolras must carry the weight of inspiration and gravity. He should be played with focus, charisma, and deep moral authority. He's not a politician but a prophet, willing to die for the future he believes in. His speeches should stir the audience, and his death should break them. He represents the dream of liberty—noble, doomed, and unforgettable.

Thénardier (40+ lines)

Thénardier is the story's most cunning and vile opportunist—a parasite who survives by exploiting others, always angling for profit, power, or escape. In the novel, he is both comic and grotesque: a master of deception, cowardice, and cruelty. On stage, Thénardier must be played with theatrical flair but never cartoonish. He's dangerous beneath the humor—a rat dressed in a gentleman's rags. His manipulation of the poor, his abuse of children, and his attempts to blackmail Valjean reveal a deeply self-serving man without a moral compass. He is the story's dark mirror of society's failure: clever, unscrupulous, and always watching for his next opportunity.

Madame Thénardier (70+ lines)

Madame Thénardier is just as cruel and greedy as her husband, though more grounded in brute survival. In the novel, she is a harsh, domineering mother who abuses Cosette and supports her husband's schemes with blind loyalty. On stage, she should be portrayed with raw energy and menace, blending hardened realism with biting sarcasm. While Thénardier plots, she reinforces his cruelty through physicality and intimidation. Together, they form a grotesque caricature of parental authority gone wrong. Her role should feel both comedic and chilling—a woman shaped by desperation, who has allowed bitterness to eclipse any remaining humanity.

Bishop Myriel - The Bishop of Digne (35+ lines)

The Bishop is the spark that changes the course of Jean Valjean's life. In the novel, he is portrayed with warmth, humility, and an almost saint-like compassion. He sees past Valjean's crime and offers him dignity instead of punishment. On stage, the Bishop should be played with stillness and gentle authority—radiating a deep, quiet love that doesn't need to prove itself. His presence is brief, but his impact echoes through the entire story. He embodies divine grace: the possibility that kindness can break the cycle of sin. His candlesticks become the symbol of redemption, passed from hand to hand like a sacred torch.

Father Fauchelevent (10+ lines)

Father Fauchelevent is a humble gardener-turned-monk whose life is saved by Jean Valjean early in the novel, creating a debt of gratitude that later allows Valjean to find refuge in the convent. He represents quiet redemption—an ordinary man who, through grace and loyalty, becomes a vessel of safety and kindness. On stage, Fauchelevent should be portrayed with warmth, simplicity, and a touch of endearing awkwardness. His genuine concern for Valjean and Cosette contrasts with the world's cruelty, reminding the audience that goodness often comes from unexpected places.

ADDITIONAL ROLES

Mademoiselle Baptistine: Bishop Myriel's sister. Calm. Tries to always please brother.

Madame Magloire: Housekeeper for the bishop and his sister. A tad scattered.

Madame Victurnien: Runs the female side of the factory. She is a self-righteous, pious widow who becomes aware of Fantine's secret child through gossip and driven by her own sense of morality, ensures Fantine's dismissal from the factory.

Marguerite: Fantine's neighbor in Montreuil-sur-Mer. She is a poor, devout, and charitable woman who becomes Fantine's confidante.

Jacquin Labarre: (male or female) Landlord of the inn

Husband: A man interested in protecting his family.

Wife: A woman interested in protecting her family.

Marquise de R: The good woman, who was well worthy of the name. Although Hugo does not finish her name for us.

Gervais: One of those gay and gentle children, who go from land to land affording a view of their knees through the holes in their trousers.

Sister Simplicity: A nun known for her unwavering truthfulness and compassion. Cares for Fantine on her deathbed.

Zéphine, Dahlia, Favourite: Female friends of Fantine

Felix Tholomyès: Fantine's love interest.

Blachevelle, Listolier, Fameuil: Friends of Felix Tholomyès, Fantine's love interest

Jacque: Jean Valjean/Monsieur Madeleine's personal assistant.

Bamatabois: A man of high society. An idler of the town who torments Fantine by putting snow down her back.

President: A Judge/Official

Court Official: Reads the accusation at hand.

Prosecutor: A Court Official

Cochepaille: Convict for life. No less savage and seemed even more stupid than the other prisoners. He was one of those wretched men whom nature has sketched out for wild beasts, and on whom society puts the finishing touches as convicts in the galleys.

Chenildieu: A prisoner for life, as was indicated by his red cassock and his green cap. He was serving out his sentence at the galleys of Toulon, whence he had been brought for this case. He was a small man of about fifty, brisk, wrinkled, frail, yellow, brazen-faced, feverish, who had a sort of sickly feebleness about all his limbs and his whole person, and an immense force in his glance.

Champmathieu: The man accused to be Jean Valjean, he seems to be at least sixty; there was something indescribably coarse, stupid, and frightened about him.

Brevet: The ex-convict wore the black and gray waistcoat of the central prisons. Brevet was a person sixty years of age, who had a sort of businessman's face, and the air of a rascal.

Alice: Member of the ABC. A strong female character.

ENSEMBLE

Workers in the Factory, Townspeople of Digne and Montfermeil, Guards, Priest and Nuns, Debtors, Landlady, Jurors, Court Observers, Inn People, Revolutionists.

SCENE LIST

ACT 1

SCENE 1 ~ Toulon Prison

A bleak prison intake area. Harsh light. INMATES file toward a desk to receive release papers. The atmosphere is rigid and quiet, broken only by the clinking of chains and distant barking of orders. COCHEPAILLE, CHENILDIEU, and BREVET stand aside. Others are processing out.

COCHEPAILLE: From year to year our souls have dried away slowly. When the heart is dry, the eye is dry.

CHENILDIEU: ahh- Jean Valjean's departure from the galleys, it had been nineteen years since he had shed a tear. Aren't you going to miss us Valjean??

BREVET: Jean Valjean entered the galleys sobbing and trembling; he left hardened. He entered in despair; he left sullen.

INMATES: What had happened within his soul?

JAVERT: *(to GUARD)* All animals are to be found in men, and each of them exists in some man, sometimes several at a time. *(to JEAN VALJEAN)* Number?

JEAN VALJEAN: 24601.

JAVERT: Name?

JEAN VALJEAN: You know my name! You know my crime—nineteen years for taking a loaf of bread.

JAVERT: *(coy)* Ah, ah, ah… Five years for stealing a loaf of bread, fourteen years for trying to escape. You criminals are all the same. Trying to make light of your actions. You can't even answer a simple question without rebelling. Clearly, you have learned nothing.

JEAN VALJEAN: My sister's children were starving!

JAVERT: And what about the baker's window?! I consider all crimes essentially equal, and equally worthy of punishment.

JEAN VALJEAN: I would have paid.

JAVERT: The law is the law. Name?

JEAN VALJEAN: Jean Valjean. Am I free?

JAVERT: Liberation is not deliverance. A convict may leave the galleys behind, but not his crime. You will carry this yellow passport wherever you go. It marks you, convict. Show your papers, whether you are asked for them or not. Failure to show your papers is a breach of parole. Break your parole and you will end up here again. Next time the sentence will be life.

JEAN VALJEAN: I will never return to this place.

JAVERT: *(to GUARD)* That is what they all say.

> *Chains clink as JEAN VALJEAN steps away slowly. Lights dim slightly to indicate scene change.*

SCENE 2 ~ Digne

A traveler enters the little town of Digne. He doesn't go unnoticed. He has a wretched appearance: medium stature, thickset and robust, in the prime of life—perhaps forty-six or forty-eight years old. A cap with a drooping leather visor partly conceals his face, burned and tanned by sun and wind, dripping with perspiration. His shirt of coarse yellow linen is fastened at the neck by a small silver anchor, revealing a hairy chest. He wears a twisted cravat, worn blue trousers, a tattered gray blouse patched with green cloth, a new soldier's knapsack, and carries a knotty stick. His shaved head and long beard complete the picture.

TOWNSPERSON 1: Do you know him?

TOWNSPERSON 2: Evidently, he's only a passer-by.

TOWNSPERSON 3: Where do you think he came from?

TOWNSPERSON 4: From the south; from the seashore, perhaps?

TOWNSPERSON 5: He must have been walking all day. Look at him! He seems very much fatigued.

TOWNSPERSON 6: I saw him pause beneath the trees of the boulevard.

TOWNSPERSON 7: He must have been very thirsty: my children followed him and saw him stop again for a drink, at the fountain in the marketplace.

JEAN VALJEAN pulls off his cap and humbly salutes a GENDARME. The GENDARME does not return the salute, but instead stares attentively, then enters the town hall. JEAN VALJEAN enters an inn—The Cross of Colbas.
The HOST, JACQUIN LABARRE, hears the door open and speaks without looking up.

JACQUIN LABARRE: What do you wish, sir?

JEAN VALJEAN: Food and lodging.

JACQUIN LABARRE: Nothing easier. *(Turning his head and inspecting JEAN VALJEAN)* As long as you pay for it.

JEAN VALJEAN: I have money. *(reaches for his purse)*

JACQUIN LABARRE: In that case, we are at your service.

While JEAN VALJEAN warms himself, JACQUIN LABARRE tears a scrap of newspaper, writes on it, and gives it to a CHILD, who runs to the town hall. JEAN VALJEAN puts his purse back in his pocket, removes his knapsack, sets it near the door, keeps his stick, and sits near the fire.

JEAN VALJEAN: Will dinner be ready soon?

JACQUIN LABARRE: Immediately.

TOWNSPERSON 1: *(to an INNPERSON)* Did you see that man over there?

TOWNSPERSON 2: *(to an INNPERSON)* Clearly, he's not from around here.

TOWNSPERSON 1: I heard he took water from a child at the fountain.

INNPERSON: *(to another group)* See that man over there, stay clear!

JEAN VALJEAN: Will dinner be ready soon?

JACQUIN LABARRE: Soon...

> *The CHILD returns. JACQUIN LABARRE reads the note, frowns, and approaches JEAN VALJEAN.*

JACQUIN LABARRE: I cannot receive you, sir.

JEAN VALJEAN: *(half rising)* What! Are you afraid that I will not pay you? Do you want me to pay in advance? I have money, I tell you.

JACQUIN LABARRE: It is not that.

JEAN VALJEAN: What then?

JACQUIN LABARRE: I... have no room.

JEAN VALJEAN: *(calmly)* Put me in the stable.

JACQUIN LABARRE: I cannot.

JEAN VALJEAN: Why?

JACQUIN LABARRE: The horses take up all the space.

JEAN VALJEAN: Very well! A corner of the loft then, a truss of straw. We will see about that after dinner.

JACQUIN LABARRE: I cannot give you any dinner.

JEAN VALJEAN: Ah! Bah! But I am dying of hunger. I have been walking since sunrise. I have travelled twelve leagues. I pay. I wish to eat.

JACQUIN LABARRE: I have nothing… nothing for *you*.

JEAN VALJEAN: Nothing! And all that?

JACQUIN LABARRE: All that is engaged by my customers.

JEAN VALJEAN: *(sits back down)* I am a customer. There is enough food there for twenty. I am at an inn; I am hungry, and I will stay.

JACQUIN LABARRE: *(leans in, irritated)* You don't understand. I said, go away!

> *A couple CUSTOMERS leave. JEAN VALJEAN stirs the fire with his staff. JACQUIN LABARRE stares him down and lowers his voice.*

JACQUIN LABARRE: Stop! You are going to frighten my customers. Do you want me to tell you who you are? I know who you are. And I know where you came from, Jean Valjean. When I saw you come in, I suspected something. I sent to the town hall, and this was the reply... Can you read?

JEAN VALJEAN: I see.

JACQUIN LABARRE: I am in the habit of being polite to everyone. But you should go!

> *JEAN VALJEAN drops his head, retrieves his belongings, and leaves. The inn's guests and*

bystanders whisper, pointing at him as he disappears into the town.

JEAN VALJEAN: *(to self, amid LOOKERS' whispers)* Do not turn around. People who are crushed do not look behind them. They know but too well the evil fate which follows them. *(SFX: thunderclap)* I must find shelter… Lord, is there no place for me? Will no one receive me? Perhaps a home…

He sees a FAMILY through a window—HUSBAND laughing, CHILD giggling, WIFE smiling.

JEAN VALJEAN: *(quietly)* Perhaps they did not hear me? *(knocks again)*

WIFE: It seems to me, husband, that someone is knocking.

HUSBAND: No… it's just the wind on the windowpane.

A third knock. The HUSBAND comes to the door.

JEAN VALJEAN: Pardon me, sir. Could you, in consideration of payment, give me a plate of soup and a corner of that shed yonder in the garden, in which to sleep? I'd be happy to pay.

HUSBAND: Who are you?

JEAN VALJEAN: I have just come from… I have walked all day long. I have travelled twelve leagues. Can you please help me?

HUSBAND: I would not refuse to lodge any respectable man. But why do you not go to the inn?

JEAN VALJEAN: There is no room.

HUSBAND: Bah! Impossible. Have you been…

JEAN VALJEAN: No one will receive me… please.

HUSBAND: Are you the man—

He grabs a gun.

JEAN VALJEAN: *(gently)* Ah! You know? —

WIFE: *(clutching children)* He's dangerous!

HUSBAND: Clear out!

WIFE: Children, come!

JEAN VALJEAN: For pity's sake, a glass of water… please, I don't mean any harm.

HUSBAND: Leave us. I won't hesitate to protect my family!

The door slams. Bolts are heard locking. A shutter slams. JEAN VALJEAN wanders the street. He sees a PRISON guarded by a GENDARME.

JEAN VALJEAN: Ah, a prison. Am I so desperate I want to be inside those bars again? Perhaps for just one night, just for some rest, a plate of food. *(Removing his cap politely)* Excuse me, would you have kindness… give me lodging for the night?

GENDARME 2: The prison is not an inn. Get arrested, and we'll gladly welcome you.

JEAN VALJEAN: *(turns away)* Very well. I wasn't sure how I would feel back inside those bars anyway. Ah, here's some straw. Perhaps this could keep me warm… *(SFX: DOG BARKING)* Are you kidding me?!

Am I not even fit to sleep with a dog?! *(shakes fist at the Lord)* Fine! Here, a bench, a cold stone bench.

An OLD WOMAN exits a nearby church.

MARQUISE DE R: What are you doing there, my friend?

JEAN VALJEAN: *(harshly)* As you see, my good woman, I am sleeping… or trying.

MARQUISE DE R: On this bench?

JEAN VALJEAN: I have had a mattress of wood for nineteen years—today I have a mattress of stone.

MARQUISE DE R: You are cold and hungry, no doubt. Here… I have only four sous in my purse. Someone might have given you a lodging out of charity.

JEAN VALJEAN: I have knocked at all doors. I have been driven away everywhere.

She touches his arm and points across the street.

MARQUISE DE R: You have knocked at all doors?

JEAN VALJEAN: Yes.

MARQUISE DE R: Have you knocked at that one? Their light is still on.

JEAN VALJEAN: No.

MARQUISE DE R: Knock there.

SCENE 3 ~ The Bishop

MADEMOISELLE BAPTISINE and MADAME
MAGLOIRE set the table and prepare for a late
dinner.

MADAME MAGLOIRE: Is the good Bishop still
working?

MADEMOISELLE BAPTISTINE: You know he is
hard at work on writing his book.

MADAME MAGLOIRE: *(trying to control herself)*
Well, while we wait, I had heard some news in town…
People have spoken of a prowler… of evil appearance; a
suspicious vagabond has arrived!! He could be
anywhere!

MADEMOISELLE BAPTISTINE: Nonsense! Our
community is quick to come to accusations and
judgment.

MADAME MAGLOIRE: We must take warning! We
don't want an unpleasant encounter! It would behoove
wise people to play the part of their own police, and to
guard themselves well, and perhaps we should bar and
barricade and fasten the doors!!

BISHOP enters while MADAME MAGLOIRE is
speaking. He warms himself by the fire.

MADEMOISELLE BAPTISTINE: Brother, did you
hear what Madame Magloire said?

BISHOP: Come, what is the matter? Let me guess… we
are in great danger!?

MADAME MAGLOIRE: It appears that a Bohemian, a barefooted vagabond is in the town!! He had presented himself at the Inn to obtain lodgings, a gallows-bird with a terrible face.

BISHOP: Whom man kills God restores to life; whom the brothers pursue the Father redeems. We must pray and believe…

MADAME MAGLOIRE: Bishop Myriel, we must lock our doors!

BISHOP: Really?!

MADAME MAGLOIRE: Yes, Monseigneur. That is how it is *(looking out the window)*. There will be some sort of catastrophe in this town to-night. Just you wait! Everyone says so!! And with the police so badly regulated… the idea of living in a mountainous country and not even having lights in the streets at night! It's black as ovens out there! And I say, Good Bishop, Mademoiselle agrees—

MADEMOISELLE BAPTISTINE: I say nothing.

MADAME MAGLOIRE: We say that this house is not safe at all; perhaps you will permit me to go to the locksmith, so he can replace the ancient locks on the doors. I say that nothing is more terrible than a door which can be opened from the outside; and I say that we need bolts, Monseigneur! Bolts! If only for this night! Moreover, Monseigneur has the habit of always saying, "Come in."

A tolerably violent knock is heard on the door.

BISHOP: Come in.

The door opens. JEAN VALJEAN enters, advances
a step, and halts, leaving the door open behind him.
He has his knapsack on his shoulders, his cudgel in
his hand, a rough, audacious, weary, and violent
expression in his eyes. The fire on the hearth lights
him up. MADAME MAGLOIRE trembles.
MADEMOISELLE BAPTISTINE starts up in terror,
then watches her brother. The BISHOP fixes a
tranquil eye on the man.

JEAN VALJEAN: See here. My name is Jean Valjean.
I was a convict from the galleys. I was liberated four
days ago. I have been walking for four days since I left
Toulon. I have travelled a dozen leagues today on foot. I
have tried to stay at multiple places, no one wants a man
like me in their presence.

MADAME MAGLOIRE: *(under breath)* I can
understand why…

BISHOP: All people are created in the image of God, no
matter how far they have fallen within the social
hierarchy of this world.

JEAN VALJEAN: No one will take me. What is this
place? I have money—savings, which I earned in the
galleys by my labor, in the course of nineteen years. I
will pay. I am very hungry. Are you willing that I should
remain?

BISHOP: Madame Magloire, you will set another place,
please.

JEAN VALJEAN: Stop. Did you hear? I am a galley-
slave; a convict. *(Presents a large sheet of yellow
paper.)* Here's my passport. This serves to expel me

from every place where I go. Will you read it? I know how to read. I learned in the galleys. There is a school there for those who choose to learn. Hold, this is what they put on this passport: *(hands over yellow paper)*

BISHOP: *(skimming, only reading underlined words)* Jean Valjean, <u>discharged convict</u>, native of— has been <u>nineteen years</u> in the galleys: five years for <u>house-breaking and burglary</u>; fourteen years for having <u>attempted to escape on four occasions</u>. He is a very <u>dangerous man</u>.

JEAN VALJEAN: There! Everyone has cast me out. Is this an inn? Will you give me something to eat and a bed? Have you a stable?

BISHOP: Madame Magloire, you will put white sheets on the bed in the alcove.

MADAME MAGLOIRE: Right away.

BISHOP: Sit down, sir, and warm yourself. We are going to eat in a few moments, and your bed will be prepared while you are eating.

JEAN VALJEAN: *(stupefied)* Really? What! You will keep me? A convict! You call me sir!? Most people say, "Get out of here, you dog!" I felt sure that you would expel me, so I told you at once who I am. Oh, what a good woman that was who directed me hither! A bed with a mattress and sheets, like the rest of the world! It has been nineteen years since I have slept in a bed! You are good people. Pardon me, monsieur innkeeper, but what is your name? You are a fine man. You are an innkeeper, are you not?

BISHOP: I am a priest who lives here.

JEAN VALJEAN: A priest! Oh, what a fine priest! Then you are not going to demand any money of me? You are the curé of this church, are you not?! I am a fool, truly! I had not perceived your skull-cap.

As he speaks, he deposits his knapsack and cudgel in a corner and seats himself.

JEAN VALJEAN: You are humane, Monsieur le Curé; you have not scorned me. A good priest is a very good thing. Then you do not require me to pay?

BISHOP: No, keep your money.

MADAME MAGLOIRE returns with a silver fork and spoon and places them on the table.

BISHOP: *(gently and polished)* Madame Magloire, place those things as near the fire as possible. The night wind is harsh on the Alps. You must be cold, sir. Here, this lamp gives a very bad light.

MADAME MAGLOIRE understands him and goes to get the two silver candlesticks. JEAN VALJEAN is given a plate of food.

JEAN VALJEAN: Monsieur le Curé, you are too good; you do not despise me? You receive me into your house, and you light your candles for me?

BISHOP: This is not my house; it is the house of Jesus Christ. This door does not demand of him who enters whether he has a name. You suffer; you are hungry and thirsty; you are welcome.

JEAN VALJEAN: Thank you.

BISHOP: Do not thank me. Everything here is yours. What need have I to know your name? Besides, before you told me, I knew yours.

JEAN VALJEAN: *(astonished)* Really? You knew what I was called?

BISHOP: Yes, you are called my brother.

JEAN VALJEAN: Stop, Monsieur le Curé, I was very hungry when I entered here; but you are so good, that I no longer know what has happened to me.

BISHOP: You have suffered much?

JEAN VALJEAN: A plank to sleep on, the thrashings, the double chain for nothing. Dogs, dogs are happier!

BISHOP: Yes, you have come from a very sad place. Listen. There will be more joy in heaven over the tear-bathed face of a repentant sinner than over the white robes of a hundred just men. If you emerge from that sad place with thoughts of hatred and of wrath against mankind, you are deserving of pity; if you emerge with thoughts of goodwill and of peace, you are more worthy than any one of us.

MADEMOISELLE BAPTISTINE: You must be tired, Monsieur.

BISHOP: Sister, I will escort our guest to his room. Can you hand me a candlestick?

> *BISHOP takes one of the two silver candlesticks from MADEMOISELLE BAPTISTINE, from the table, and hands the other to his guest. MADAME MAGLOIRE puts away the silverware in the cupboard.*

JEAN VALJEAN: Ah! really! You lodge me in your house, close to yourself like this? How do you know that I have not been an assassin?

BISHOP: That is the concern of the good God. No one has ever seen God, but if we love each other, God lives in us, and His love is brought to full expression in us. May you pass a good night. Tomorrow morning, before you set out, you shall drink a cup of warm milk from our cows. *(Moving his lips like one who is praying, he raises two fingers of his right hand and bestows his benediction on the man.)*

> *LIGHTS OUT.*
> *The next morning... at sunrise. LIGHTS UP.*

MADAME MAGLOIRE: *(frantic)* Mademoiselle Baptistine, Mademoiselle! Do you know where the silver basket is?

MADEMOISELLE BAPTISTINE: Isn't it where you put it last night? *(in a tizzy)*

MADAME MAGLOIRE: Monseigneur, Monseigneur! Does your Grace know where the basket is?

BISHOP: Yes.

MADAME MAGLOIRE: Jesus the Lord be blessed! I did not know what had become of it.

MADEMOISELLE BAPTISTINE: Where is it?

> *BISHOP picks up the empty basket (in a flowerbed).*

BISHOP: Here it is. It's empty.

MADAME MAGLOIRE: What?? Nothing in it!

MADEMOISELLE BAPTISTINE: Where's the silver?

BISHOP: Ah, so it is the silver which troubles you? I don't know where it is.

MADAME MAGLOIRE: Good God! It is stolen! That man who was here last night has stolen it. (*Runs inside and comes back out.*) Monseigneur, the man is gone! The silver has been stolen! Ah, the abomination! He has stolen our silver!

BISHOP: (*remained silent for a moment; then he raised his grave eyes, and said gently*) Ladies, ladies, was that silver ours? Madame Magloire, I have for a long time detained it belongs to the poor. Who was that man? A poor man, evidently.

MADAME MAGLOIRE: Alas, it is not for my sake, nor for Mademoiselle's. It makes no difference to us. But it is for the sake of Monseigneur. What is Monseigneur to eat with now?

BISHOP: (*gazed at her with an air of amazement*) Ah, come! Are there no such things as pewter forks and spoons?

MADAME MAGLOIRE: (*shrugged her shoulders*) Pewter has an odor.

BISHOP: Iron forks and spoons, then.

MADAME MAGLOIRE: (*made an expressive grimace*) Iron has a taste.

BISHOP: Very well, wooden ones then.

MADEMOISELLE BAPTISTINE: There. There. We will make do.

MADAME MAGLOIRE: (*to self*) A pretty idea, truly, to take in a man like that! He could have killed us! How fortunate that he did nothing but steal! You shouldn't have said, come in.

SFX: *Knock at the door.*

BISHOP: Come in.

Door opens. Three GENDARMES holding JEAN VALJEAN by the collar. A brigadier of gendarmes, in command of the group, was standing near the door. He entered and advanced to the BISHOP, making a military salute. JEAN VALJEAN, dejected, raised his head with an air of stupefaction.

GENDARME: Monseigneur—

JEAN VALJEAN: (*murmured*) Monseigneur! So, he is not the curé?

GENDARME: Silence! He is Monseigneur the Bishop. Good Bishop, we found this convict outside of town with your things…

BISHOP: Ah! Here you are, friend! I am glad to see you. Well, but how is this? I gave you the candlesticks too, and for which you can certainly get two hundred francs. Why did you not carry them away with your forks and spoons?

GENDARME: Monseigneur, so what this man said is true, then? We came across him. He was walking like a man who was running away. We stopped him to look into the matter. He had this silver—

BISHOP: And he told you, (*with a smile*), that it had been given to him by a kind old fellow of a priest with whom he had passed the night? I see how the matter stands. And you have brought him back here? It is a mistake.

GENDARME: In that case, we can let him go?

BISHOP: Certainly. Officers, you may be excused. *(GENDARMES leave.)* My friend, before you go, here are your candlesticks. Take them. *(He takes the two silver candlesticks and brings them to JEAN VALJEAN. The two women looked on without uttering a word, without a gesture.)*

JEAN VALJEAN: But...

BISHOP: It's time you forgive yourself, and the world if you can. Promise you will do what I ask.

JEAN VALJEAN: Yes, Father.

BISHOP: Remember, you no longer belong to what is evil, but what is good. Now, go in peace. By the way, when you return, my friend, it is not necessary to pass through the garden. You can always enter and depart through the street door. It is never fastened with anything but a latch, either by day or by night. (*draws near to him and says in a low voice: —*) Do not forget, never forget, that you have promised to use this money in becoming an honest man. Jean Valjean, my brother, you no longer belong to evil, but to good. It is your soul that I buy from you today; I give you to God.

JEAN VALJEAN, upset, walks off.

SCENE 4 ~ Little Gervais

JEAN VALJEAN leaves the town as though he were fleeing from it. He sets out at a very hasty pace through the fields, without perceiving that he is incessantly retracing his steps. He sits down behind a bush. In the middle of this meditation, a joyous sound becomes audible... GERVAIS hums or sings a simple tune. Without stopping his song, GERVAIS halts in his march from time to time, and plays at knucklebones with some coins which he has in his hand—his whole fortune, probably. Among this money there is one forty-sou piece. He halts beside the bush, without perceiving JEAN VALJEAN, and tosses up his handful of sous, which, up to that time, he has caught with a good deal of adroitness on the back of his hand. This time the forty-sou piece escapes him, and rolls toward JEAN VALJEAN, who sets his foot upon it. GERVAIS looks after his coin and catches sight of him. Shows no astonishment and walks straight up to JEAN VALJEAN.

GERVAIS: (with childish confidence) Sir, my money.

JEAN VALJEAN: What is your name?

GERVAIS: Little Gervais, sir.

JEAN VALJEAN: Go away.

GERVAIS: Sir, give me back my money.

JEAN VALJEAN drops his head and makes no reply.

GERVAIS: My money, sir. (*JEAN VALJEAN does not look up.*) My piece of money! (*yells*) My white piece! My silver! (*Grabs him by the collar of his blouse and shakes him. At the same time he makes an effort to displace the big iron-shod shoe which rests on his treasure.*) I want my piece of money! It's my forty sous!

> *The child weeps. JEAN VALJEAN raises his head. He still remains seated. His eyes are troubled. He gazes at the child, in a sort of amazement, then he stretches out his hand toward his cudgel and cries in a terrible voice...*

JEAN VALJEAN: Who's there?

GERVAIS: (*pleading*) I, sir. Little Gervais! I! Give me back my forty sous, if you please! Take your foot away, sir, if you please! Come now, will you take your foot away? Take your foot away, please!

JEAN VALJEAN: Ah! It's still you! (*rising abruptly to his feet, his foot still resting on the silver piece*) Take off, will you. Go!

> *The frightened child looks at him, runs off. JEAN VALJEAN watches him off into the distance. He settles his cap more firmly on his brow, advances a step and stops to look at the coin. At that moment he catches sight of the forty-sou piece, which his foot has half ground into the earth, and which is shining among the pebbles. It is as though he has received a galvanic shock.*

BISHOP: (*off stage*) No one has ever seen God, but if we love each other, God lives in us, and His love is brought to full expression in us.

JEAN VALJEAN: What have I done? (*looks up, goes after*) Little Gervais! Little Gervais! (*He pauses and waits. There is no reply. He sets out, then he begins to run*) Little Gervais! Little Gervais!

He enters a village. A few NUNS and some people walk by.

JEAN VALJEAN: *(urgent)* Have you seen a child pass?

PRIEST/NUN 1: No.

JEAN VALJEAN: One named Little Gervais?

PRIEST/NUN 1: *(looks at others, confused)* We have seen no child.

JEAN VALJEAN draws two five-franc pieces from his bag and hands them to the nuns.

JEAN VALJEAN: This is for your poor people. Please, he was a little lad, about ten years old. One of those Savoyards, from the mountains, you know?

TOWNSPERSON/NUN 2: We have not seen him.

JEAN VALJEAN: Little Gervais?? There are no Savoyards here? Can you tell me?

TOWNSPERSON/NUN 3: If he is like what you say, my friend, he is a little stranger. Such persons pass through these parts. We know nothing of him.

JEAN VALJEAN seizes two more coins of five francs each with violence and gives them.

JEAN VALJEAN: For your poor. You should have me arrested. I am a thief.

*The group moves on, much alarmed. JEAN
VALJEAN sets out in the direction which he had
first taken.*

JEAN VALJEAN: Little Gervais! Little Gervais! Little
Gervais! (*His shout dies away in the mist, without even
awakening an echo. He murmurs yet once more*) Little
Gervais!

*It is his last effort; his legs give way abruptly under
him, as though an invisible power has suddenly
overwhelmed him with the weight of his evil
conscience; he falls exhausted.*

JEAN VALJEAN: I am a wretch!

*Then his heart bursts, and he begins to cry. It is the
first time in nineteen years.*

BISHOP: *(off stage)* You have promised me to become
an honest man. You must continue to give yourself to
Him.

SCENE 5 ~ Fantine

FANTINE enters singing/humming a tune. She holds a carpet bag and is dressed like a workingwoman inclined to turn into a peasant again. She is young. Was she handsome? Perhaps, but in that attire, it is not apparent. Her hair, a golden lock of which has escaped, seems very thick, but is severely concealed beneath an ugly, tight, close, nun-like cap, tied under the chin. A smile would display beautiful teeth; but she does not smile. She is pale and appears weary and rather sickly.

FANTINE: We can play here just for a little while, Cosette. Just for a little bit. Go on.

MADAME THÉNARDIER enters, humming (out of tune). FANTINE stands quietly with her carpet bag, watching her child play. She coughs now and then. THÉNARDIER enters but keeps his distance.

MADAME THÉNARDIER: There, there girls, play nicely. Éponine, look after Azelma! Look there, you can play with that sweet little blonde girl there *(to self, disgusted with her beautiful looks)* isn't she beautiful… play nice now girls. Show her how you can be friends.

FANTINE: You have two beautiful children there, Madame.

MADAME THÉNARDIER: Aren't they though? I have not seen you or your beautiful child here before. What brings you here, to Montfermeil? Has your husband found work here?

FANTINE: My daughter and I are just passing through. I am looking for work. Your girls look so happy… visions of joy.

MADAME THÉNARDIER: You didn't mention a husband, you poor dear. You're all alone… just you and that beautiful, beautiful child?

FANTINE nods yes.

MADAME THÉNARDIER: You brave, sweet young thing. Here, sit with me, while we watch our children. My name is Madame Thénardier. My husband and I keep the Inn over there. Tell me your troubles.

FANTINE: Thank you, kindly, I am fatigued.

MADAME THÉNARDIER: Where are you traveling from? Let me guess… *(looks intrigued)* Paris??

[FLASHBACK…]

FANTINE: Blachevelle loved Favourite; Listolier adored Dahlia, who had taken for her nickname the name of a flower; Fameuio idolized Zéphine; Felix had me, he called me Blonde, because of my sunny hair.

THÉNARDIERS pause. GIRLS enter calling to FANTINE who sits trying to decide if she should join.

DAHLIA: Come, Fantine! Don't be long!

ZÉPHINE: I wonder what our gentlemen will bring us?

DAHLIA: It will certainly be something pretty?

FAVOURITE: I want it to be of gold. *(looks at finger)*

ZÉPHINE: Chocolates?

DAHLIA: A fancy dress.

ZÉPHINE: Come on, Fantine. Fancy up, your Felix is about to be here. *(offers her a fashionable hat, lipstick, etc)*

DAHLIA: Really, Fantine, the Paris men are looking for ladies! *(GIRLS giggle)*

FANTINE: This is who I am.

FAVOURITE: Yes, the prize of modesty.

> *GIRLS continue to spruce up. MUSIC begins. FELIX, BLACHEVELLE, LISTOLIER, and FAMEUIL enter with a flower for each. A DANCE begins...*

FELIX: Come my sweet...

> *After the dance, the four merry couples, mingled with the sun. And in this community of Paradise, talking, singing, running, dancing, chasing butterflies, they all receive, to some extent, the kisses of all, with the exception of FANTINE, who is hedged about with that vague resistance of hers composed of dreaminess and wildness, and who is in love. The GIRLS separate from the MEN*

FAVOURITE: Fantine, you have a curious look about you.

ZÉPHINE: She's in love.

DAHLIA: Such things are joys. *(speaking of the MEN)*

ZÉPHINE: Ladies we must be profound... we appeal to life and nature.

FAVOURITE: ... yet make light spring forth from everything.

FANTINE: I believe the Lord created the fields and forests expressly for those in love.

GIRLS pause. GUYS talk.

BLACHEVELLE: Our beautiful women waste themselves sweetly.

LISTOLIER: They think that this will never come to an end.

FAMEUIL: Philosophers, poets, painters, observe these ecstasies and know not what to make of it, so what if such beauties are greatly dazzled by it?

FELIX draws FANTINE in. The COUPLES each exit together.

FELIX:

Badajoz is my home,
And Love is my name.
To my eyes in flame,
All my soul doth come.
For instruction meet
I receive at thy feet.

[PRESENT...]

FANTINE: For three years we lived as if we were the only things that mattered. Then one day our "gentlemen" sent us a letter, and they were gone.

MADAME THÉNARDIER: A letter… Why! For shame. You had given yourself to this man as to a husband, and you poor girl, you had a (beautiful, beautiful) child. And what is to happen to you and your precious… What's her name?

FANTINE: Cosette.

MADAME THÉNARDIER: *(to self)* Yes, Cash-set. How old is she?

FANTINE: She is going on three.

MADAME THÉNARDIER: That is the age of my eldest, my precious Éponine. Éponine, put your dress down. Show the nice lady how you can curtsy, *(boasting)* I taught her myself. No, not you Azelma!! Girls, stop pushing each other! Ahhh—Notice how easily our children got acquainted?! One would swear that they were three sisters!

FANTINE: *(hesitant at first)* Yes… sisters… Madame, would you… could you keep my child for me?

MADAME THÉNARDIER: What!? Me?

FANTINE: You see, I cannot take my daughter. My work will not permit it. With a child with me, *(slight cough)* one can find no situation. It was the good God who caused me to pass your inn. When I caught sight of your little ones, so pretty, so clean, and so happy, it overwhelmed me. I said: 'Here is a good mother. That is just the thing; that will make three sisters.' And then, it will not be long before I return. Will you keep my child for me?

MADAME THÉNARDIER: Hmm—

FANTINE: I will give you six francs a month.

THÉNARDIER enters the conversation. He's been eavesdropping, talking to people in the town.

THÉNARDIER: Not for less than seven francs. And six months paid in advance. Six times seven makes… *(tries to do the math)*

FANTINE: Done.

MADAME THÉNARDIER: … forty-two… my husband…

FANTINE: I will give it.

THÉNARDIER: And fifteen francs in addition for preliminary expenses.

MADAME THÉNARDIER: Total, fifty-seven francs.

FANTINE: I will pay it. I have eighty francs.

MADAME THÉNARDIER: We'll take that. And the carpet bag. We will want your darling daughter to look her best.

FANTINE: I shall travel on foot. I shall earn money, and as soon as I have a little I will return for my darling.

MADAME THÉNARDIER: That sounds like a perfect plan.

FANTINE: I will go and say goodbye to my dear sweet Cosette…

FANTINE exits.

THÉNARDIER: You played the mousetrap nicely…

MADAME THÉNARDIER: With the help of our precious Éponine and Azelma. Fantine didn't suspect a thing. And soon instead of a playmate, they will have their own servant.

SCENE 6 ~ Montfermeil

From Jean Valjean to Father Madeleine

A workhouse is present. MEN on one side. LADIES on the other. JEAN VALJEAN enters and sits at his desk. MADAME VICTURNIEN watches over the ladies. JACQUE watches over the men. JAVERT enters. JACQUE greets him.

JACQUE: Good afternoon, your excellency. With what do we have the pleasure of greeting you? None of our workers are in trouble, are they? We only hire…

WORKERS: …good and honest workers.

JAVERT: *(stone-faced, uninterested)* Good day. I am here to introduce myself to the owner of the factory. I am the Chief of Police here in Montfermeil, I have yet to meet him. I was told he is also the mayor of this (pathetic) town.

JACQUE: Oh, yes, sir. Let me see if he's available. Your name, sir?

JAVERT: Inspector Javert.

JACQUE: Of course, sir. *(JACQUE enters the office of JEAN VALJEAN)* Sorry to bother you, Monsieur Mayor, but an Inspector Javert is here to see you.

JEAN VALJEAN: Javert? *(to self, looks out)* Has he found me?

JACQUE: Found you, sir? I think he wants to introduce himself. He's the new chief of police. Should I let him in?

JEAN VALJEAN: Very well.

JACQUE: Right this way, Monsieur. *(leads JAVERT to JEAN VALJEAN)*

JAVERT: Good day, Monsieur Mayor. I am the new Inspector here, and I thought I would take a moment to introduce myself. Inspector Javert, at your service.

JEAN VALJEAN: *(head down, keeping busy)* Yes, well, I'm sure you will find our town quiet and uneventful. Where did you say you came from?

JAVERT: Toulon. And I assure you, if there is trouble, I will find it.

JEAN VALJEAN: It was a pleasure meeting you. I'm sorry, so very busy. Jacque will show you out.

JACQUE: Right this way.

JAVERT: I know the way out. *(Exits)*

JAVERT and FANTINE cross paths. FANTINE enters Montfermeil. TOWNSPEOPLE gather.

FANTINE: Ah, Montfermeil. I can't believe it's been 10 years since I've been here, I hardly recognize this town. *(coughs)* I keep thinking I will be able to get ahead, but then I get laid off. Perhaps here in Montfermeil, I will be able to get ahead enough to send for Cosette. *(stumbles upon a group of TOWNSPEOPLE, including FAUCHELEVENT)* Excuse me, do you know if there is any work here?

TOWNSPERSON 1: The factory over there. It produces "black goods."

FANTINE: Black goods?

TOWNSPERSON 2: *(mysterious)* Towards the close of 1815, a man, a stranger, had established himself in the town. He had been inspired with the idea of substituting gum-lac for resin, and, for bracelets in particular.

TOWNSPERSON 3: That stranger is none other than Monsieur Madeleine... now the mayor and owner of this fine factory. He went from no one to Father Madeleine to Monsieur Madeleine. Then Monsieur Madeleine became Monsieur le Maire.

TOWNSPERSON 2: *(again, mysterious)* I was once told... on the very day when he made his obscure entry into our little town, just at nightfall, on a December evening, with only a knapsack on back and thorn club in hand, a large fire had broken out in the town-hall. This man had rushed into the flames and saved, at the risk of his own life, two children who belonged to the captain of the gendarmerie; this is why they had forgotten to ask him for his passport.

FANTINE: That's quite the story.

FAUCHELEVENT: *(brings FANTINE close)* I would have died, had it not been for Father Madeleine...

FANTINE: Oh?

FAUCHELEVENT: He's strong as an ox, he is! You see, I was caught under my cart! No one could do a thing. I thought I was left to die!

FAUCHELEVENT goes to his cart.

FAUCHELEVENT: I was making my rounds, delivering goods... when I slipped and was trapped. Help! Help!

PEOPLE gather around him. JAVERT is there looking on.

TOWNSPERSON 4: Not even the police could do anything. Inspector Javert was about to watch you sink into the mud, he was. *(to FANTINE)* You want to stay clear of Inspector Javert...

FAUCHELEVENT: Help! Who is a good fellow to save an old man?

MAN 1: Has anyone got a jack?

WOMAN 1: They have gone for one.

MAN 1: How soon will it be here?

MAN 2: It will take a quarter of an hour at least.

FAUCHELEVENT: Please someone! *(JEAN VALJEAN enters)* I am being crushed!

JEAN VALJEAN: What is going on here... the man is being crushed, won't anyone help him? *(no one responds)* Listen, there is room enough still under the wagon for a man to crawl in and lift it with his back.

JAVERT: *(to self)* I have only witnessed one man in my lifetime have the strength to do what he proposes... a convict from Toulon- 24601.

JEAN VALJEAN: I will pay five louis d'ors for him. *(no response)* Ten??

MAN 3: And risk getting crushed himself!?

JEAN VALJEAN: Come! Twenty louis?!

JAVERT: It is not the goodwill they lack, but strength. It would take an incredible man to lift a wagon like that on his back.

FAUCHELEVENT: Please!! *(gasps)*

JAVERT: *(to GUARD)* Did I mention, I have only known one man able to do what he is asking. A convict, from Toulon.

FAUCHELEVENT: I'm dying! My ribs are breaking!

JEAN VALJEAN: Isn't there anybody who wants twenty louis to save this poor man's life?

FAUCHELEVENT: It's crushing me!

JEAN VALJEAN reacts and takes off his jacket.

FAUCHELEVENT: No, Father Madeleine. Go away. Not you. I must die. You can see that. Leave me. You too will be crushed.

JEAN VALJEAN lifts the cart. ALL gasp. Everyone gathers...

[PRESENT...]

FAUCHELEVENT: He was my saving grace, Father Madeleine, shifted his shoulders under the sinking cart. I tried to stop him, but he lifted my life into freedom that day, that he did.

TOWNSPERSON 5: Father Fauchelevent talks as if nothing happened in his life until he was saved by Father Madeleine…

FAUCHELEVENT: That's the way I feel. I'll be honest with you. I wasn't sure about the man… You see, before Monsieur Madeleine's arrival, everything had languished in the country; however, I was doing quite well for myself. Yet over time, I had seen this simple man grow rich, while I, a lawyer, was being ruined. This filled me with jealousy, and if I'm honest I had done all I could, on every occasion, to injure Madeleine. But then bankruptcy came; and I had nothing left but a broken cart and a dying horse. And when that cart was ready to crush me, pressing my body, sucking the life from my very being… he saved me. That's what he has done for this town likewise. I can't walk well now, because of the accident, but Monsieur le Maire bought my broken cart and my dead horse and found me a gardening job at a convent in Paris. I'm only here visiting my nephew in one of the numerous hospital beds Monsieur le Maire provided… did you know he even created a school…

FANTINE: That's a remarkable story! Does anyone know if Monsieur… the factory is hiring? And I need a place to live…

MARGUERITE: My name is Marguerite. I live in a boarding house over there. It's not luxury, but the rent is reasonable.

TOWNSPERSON 7: The factory is always hiring… as long as you are a *(emphasis)*…

ALL: good, honest worker.

TOWNSPERSON 4: You'll want to call on Madame Victurnien. She's in charge of the women's ward within the factory walls.

TOWNSPERSON 6: So, what's your story?

FANTINE: Me? I have no story. *(Begins to exit, turns back.)* But I am looking for someone to help me write a letter?

TOWNSPERSON 6: Well, why didn't you say so, step this way, dearie. *(looks back, whispers)* I'll find out her story…

SCENE 7 ~ Letters

At Thénardier's Inn. Three kids run through -
ÉPONINE, AZELMA, and GAVROCHE. COSETTE
(in rags) follows.

MADAME THÉNARDIER: Out of my Inn you filthy dogs.

ÉPONINE: Come on Azelma! Let's go outside and play.

AZELMA: Come on, Gavroche!

BOTH: *(mocking)* "Little urchin."

GAVROCHE: Hey!

MADAME THÉNARDIER: *(yelling at they run past)* Éponine, Azelma, watch over your brother. Do not let Gavroche fill his pockets with tadpoles from the sewer water again. Go outside and play. *(COSETTE also tries to walk out.)* Uh, uh, uh… not you dearie! Someone has to earn her keep… you have pots to scrub… back to work. Hopefully some customers will be here soon… if we get any customers today.

COSETTE goes back from where she came, cleans.

THÉNARDIER: Must be nice to have a servant girl to do all your work.

MADAME THÉNARDIER: It's not like I get any help from you, you lazy bum. The girl is bringing in more money than this Inn is.

THÉNARDIER: As long as her mother keeps paying…

MADAME THÉNARDIER: Fantine has a steady income. The money comes like clockwork.

THÉNARDIER: Times are tough, we now have another brat to feed.

MADAME THÉNARDIER: Trust me, I know what I'm doing. *(thinking)* Besides… I think that little urchin is developing a cough… I'm sure Fantine can set aside a few more farthings per month for her dear precious… what's her name?

THÉNARDIER: Carla?

MADAME THÉNARDIER: Cosette, you idiot!

> *LADIES in the factory. MADAME VICTURNIEN walks behind, inspecting their work, eavesdropping on the LADIES. FANTINE at the end, minding her own business.*

WORKER 1: Have you noticed Fantine, lately?

WORKER 2: Look at her over there, as if her work is better than ours.

WORKER 3: I wonder what she is thinking about… I think she looks lonely, perhaps sad.

WORKER 4: Nonsense. Fantine always has that way about her. I saw her buying a looking glass. She's beautiful. Girls beautiful like that have no right being sad.

WORKER 1: I saw her buying note paper at the stationer's shop.

WORKER 2: What for? She can't read or write!

WORKER 4: *(whispers)* Someone told me she has a child…

ALL look over at FANTINE

WORKER 3: We mustn't spread rumors… it's not our story to tell.

MADAME VICTURNIEN: Ladies, ladies! What are you ladies whispering about? Clearly you are distracted from your work. Maybe you don't need a job.

WORKERS: We do! Sorry, Madame!

MADAME VICTURNIEN: You would all be starving if it weren't for Monsieur Madeleine. You should keep your head down and be a good worker like Fantine over there.

WORKER 1: Ha! Fantine! She's slow.

WORKER 2: She's not a good person, Madame Victurnien. She's fooled you.

MADAME VICTURNIEN: What?

WORKER 4: She has a child, she does! A child and no husband!

MADAME VICTURNIEN: What? How dare Fantine fool us. Leave "Madamoiselle" Fantine to me… *(goes to FANTINE)* Fantine, *(hands her fifty francs)* this is from the mayor, you are no longer employed in this factory. In the name of Monsieur le Maire you are to leave the neighborhood.

FANTINE: This job has been a mercy from heaven, please no. What have I done? Please don't do this.

MADAME VICTURNIEN: We can't have people like you here, ruining our mayor's name.

FANTINE: I cannot leave; I paid for an apartment. I even rented furniture. Please don't do this… I… I… have a child. *(ALL gasp)* She's sick. I just got this letter, and I need to send more this month. I need to send her money. I send her money every month. She stays with an Inn Keeper and his wife.

WORKER 4: We know about you. You think you're better than us.

FANTINE: No, I don't. No. Please. I don't. Think of my child.

MADAME VICTURNIEN: Enough. This is not that kind of place. Everyone back to work. Fantine, be off with you this instant! *(Exits)*

JEAN VALJEAN: *(enters, but stays in the back)* Madame Victurnien, is everything alright in there?

MADAME VICTURNIEN: Pardon the interruption, Monsieur le Maire, I have everything under control.

SCENE 8 ~ Darkness

Split scenes - INN and TOWN and APARTMENT.

[TOWN...]

PEOPLE passing by... MAGUERITE enters... MAN and WOMAN pass by without stopping. JAVERT enters.

MARGUERITE: Flowers for sale. Buy your lady a flower?

MARGUERITE: (noticing JAVERT walking toward her) Flowers...

JAVERT: You, there. Let me see your license.

MARGUERITE: License... oh, um— *(digs in satchel)* here it is.

JAVERT: Your license to sell goods expires in just a few days. You know the law, and if you don't, I'll make sure you do.

MARGUERITE: Yes, Inspector Javert.

JAVERT: Be off with you. My city will not have vagabonds running amuck without a license. You get that taken care of or else. *(exits)*

MARGUERITE: Yes, sir.

FANTINE enters.

MARGUERITE: Fantine, what are you doing here? Aren't you supposed to be working at this time of day?

FANTINE: Oh, Marguerite! I've been let go. Madame Victurnien said Monsieur Mayor doesn't employ people like me.

MARGUERITE: You must go back to Monsieur Mayor. Does he know what that evil woman has done? He is a kind man. You are a good person.

FANTINE: Not good enough. She said the mayor dismissed me, gave me fifty francs because he is good and just. They found out about Cosette. I should be thankful. I am heading to the scribe to send the Thénardiers everything I have. My dear Cosette is sick.

MARGUERITE: Aren't you forgetting—our rent is due!? And you probably shouldn't have rented that furniture. He too will come after you!

FANTINE: I can't think of my debts. My Cosette is in need. I'll find another job. I'll sew shirts for the regiment. I need to send money to the Thénardiers, or they will throw Cosette out on the street and then what!? *(cough, cough)*

MARGUERITE: It's you I'm worried about. You really ought to see a doctor for that cough.

FANTINE: Good idea. Maybe I'll see a dentist… not a doctor. Everyone always tells me what nice teeth I have. Can I stay with you tonight?

MARGUERITE: Climb the back stairs into my room. But don't let the landlady see you or she'll kick us both out.

FANTINE: *(cough, cough)*

Inside the Thénardier Inn. MADAME THÉNARDIER holds a letter. COSETTE gathers glasses from the tables. THÉNARDIER lounges with his foot up on a table.

MADAME THÉNARDIER: Drat! This isn't the amount I asked for. Who does Fantine think she is playing with?!

THÉNARDIER: See, being the master of the house isn't so easy. Child— *(to COSETTE)* fetch me another cup of coffee. Then go get some more wood for the fire.

COSETTE: Yes, sir. (goes to get her hat, mittens, and scarf on)

MADAME THÉNARDIER: Wait! Children, come here! *(ÉPONINE, AZELMA, and GAVROCHE all come)* Winter has arrived. Aren't you all cold?

CHILDREN: Yes, momma.

MADAME THÉNARDIER: Cosette, did you hear that? My children are cold. Give them your things. Your hat, your mittens, your scarf. *(hands each item to her own children)* There. We will write your mother and let her know you have no clothing. Now get back to work, Cosette.

FANTINE wears a hat, sewing in the dark. MARGUERITE lights a candle.

MARGUERITE: Fantine, you are working yourself sick. I'm worried about you. Here, use my candle, things seem less dismal in the light.

FANTINE: No one will hire me as a servant. I have gone door to door. They all look at me with disgust. Sewing I can do… even in the dark.

MARGUERITE: You need rest.

FANTINE: Bah! I say to myself, by only sleeping five hours, and working all the rest of the time at my sewing, I shall always manage to nearly enough to earn my bread. Besides, when one is sad, one eats less. Sufferings, uneasiness, a little bread on one hand, trouble on the other—all this will support me. *(takes off her hat)*

MARGUERITE: Fantine! Your hair.

FANTINE: It was only hair, Marguerite, *(cough)* it will grow back. I was able to send ten francs to the Thénardiers. My child is no longer cold. I have clothed her with my hair. Besides, perhaps my debtors won't recognize me now. *(picks up a mirror and about to throw it away)* And I certainly have no use for this, but perhaps it's worth something to someone. Tomorrow I will see what I can make from it.

[THÉNADIER INN…]

THÉNARDIER: Ode to winter…

MADAME THÉNARDIER: Oh, you are becoming a poet now?

THÉNARDIER: Summer passed, but winter has come again. Short days, less work. Winter: no warmth, no light, no noonday, the evening joining on to the morning, fogs, twilight; the window is gray; it is impossible to see clearly at it. The sky is but a vent-hole. The whole day is a cavern. The sun has the air of a beggar. A frightful season!

AZELMA: *(enters)* Mama, a package was just delivered.

THÉNARDIER: *(opens)* Oh, look. *(holds up a skirt)* Fantine sent clothing this time. What are we supposed to do with this?

   AZELMA looks interested.

MADAME THÉNARDIER: I'll tell you what I'm going to do! Come here, Éponine, my sweet... here's a new skirt for you. Now fetch me a pen and paper.

ÉPONINE: Me? I thought Cosette was your errand girl.

MADAME THÉNARDIER: Well, she is doing the dishes now, ain't she? Now do what I asked, or you can wash your father's socks! *(AZELMA escapes the wrath)*

ÉPONINE: Yes, mam. (fetches pen and paper)

THÉNARDIER: Whatcha gunna do, my buttercup?

MADAME THÉNARDIER: *(begins writing letter)* Come here my darling daughters *(ÉPONINE and AZELMA stand near)*, this is how it's done. *(begins writing)* Cosette is ill with a malady which is going the rounds of the neighborhood. A miliary fever, they call it. Expensive drugs are required. This is ruining us, and we can no longer pay for her needs. If you do not send us

60

forty francs before the week is out, the little one will be...

[TOWN...]

Back in town... FANTINE received her letter.
PEOPLE noticing her, walking by...

FANTINE: *(talking to self, but bothered)* ...dead? No, this cannot be true. Who do they think I am? They were supposed to be good people... *(holds letter in hand, distraught, delirious all at the same time.)*

TOWNSPERSON 1: There's a girl who will come to a bad end.

MADAME VICTURNIEN: It's a good thing I put her in her place.

FANTINE: Ah! *(laughs to self)* Forty francs! The idea! Where do they think I am to get forty francs? These Thénardiers, these peasants are stupid, truly.

TOWNSPERSON 2: What makes you so happy, girl?

FANTINE: A fine piece of stupidity that some country people! *(crumples up note in fist)*

As she crossed the square, she saw a great many
PEOPLE collected around a QUACK DENTIST,
dressed in red. He was on his rounds, offering to
the public full sets of teeth, opiates, powders and
elixirs.

QUACK DENTIST: Step right up, step right up... Ahh, you, you... you my dear have beautiful teeth, you girl there, *(speaking to FANTINE)* if you want to sell me

61

your palettes, I will give you a gold napoleon apiece for them.

FANTINE: What are my palettes?

QUACK DENTIST: The palettes are the front teeth, the two upper ones.

FANTINE: How horrible!

TOWNSPERSON 4: Did you hear what he said… Two napoleons! Lucky girl!

FANTINE: No! That sounds awful!

QUACK DENTIST: *(gives her his card)* Reflect, my beauty! Two napoleons; they may prove of service. If your heart bids you; come find me. *(walks off)*

FANTINE: *(to TOWNSPERSON 5 and 6)* Can you understand such a thing? Is he not an abominable man? How can they allow such people to go about the country! Pull out my two front teeth?! Why, I should be horrible! My hair will grow again, but my teeth! Ah! What a monster of a man! I should prefer to throw myself headfirst on the pavement from the fifth story!

TOWNSPERSON 5: Yet did you hear what he offered?

FANTINE: Two napoleons!

TOWNSPERSON 6: That makes forty francs.

TOWNSPERSON 7: Yes, that makes forty francs.

FANTINE: Forty francs… Cosette? My dear little girl. Is God providing an answer? They are just teeth, right? I already pulled my back teeth. I have no hair… Let all the clouds fall upon me, and all the ocean sweep over me!

What matters it to me? I am a sponge that is already soaked. (*cough, cough*) My child will not die because of me. I will save you Cosette… *(FANTINE grips letter… runs off)*

[SEPARATE PART OF TOWN…]

Evening… outside the theater… well-to-do PEOPLE walking through…

BAMATABOIS: What a delightful evening. Of course, I'm here. Too bad the atmosphere out here isn't the same as inside… Look at what filth enters our presence…

FANTINE enters… people circle around her like she's in a dream… she's delirious…

DEBTOR: Fantine, you still owe me!! When are you going to pay?

DEBTOR 2: Pay up, Fantine.

LANDLADY: You are past due on your rent. You better start packing up your things!

MARGUERITE: You need rest Fantine…

FELIX: Fantine, what happened to you??

MADAME VICTURNIEN: Look at the wretch, it's a good thing I let her go. She's pathetic.

WORKER 1: And she thought she was better than us…

WORKER 2: Look at her now. Worthless.

WORKER 3: Unfortunate girl.

WORKER 4: She used to be beautiful.

MADAME THÉNARDIER: 100 francs, Fantine! We need more money. *(hands FANTINE a letter)*

THÉNARDIER: Your child is about to perish.

THÉNARDIER KIDS: We're hungry, there's nothing to eat!

COSETTE: Momma, help me.

ALL: *(whispers)* Misery, hunger, cold, isolation, destitution…

FANTINE: *(cough, cough)* Oh, God. Another letter. *(holds another letter)* What do they want of me? I have nothing left to give.

BAMATABOIS: My, but you are ugly. Why don't you try hiding your face. Ew! You've lost your two front teeth!!

> *FANTINE looks at him with emptiness and turns away. Taking advantage of a moment when her back is turned, he creeps up behind her with the gait of a wolf, and—stifling his laugh—bends down, picks up a handful of snow from the pavement, and thrusts it abruptly into her back, between her bare shoulders. The woman utters a roar, whirls round, gives a leap like a panther, and hurls herself upon the man, burying her nails in his face. A CROWD gathers, hooting and applauding. OFFICERS enter, as well as JAVERT. THÉNARDIERS and MARGUERITE exit.*

JAVERT: Halt. What is the meaning of this?

> *FANTINE falls down, motionless and mute, crouching like a terrified dog.*

BAMATABOIS: Did you see? Did you see? This pathetic little creature attacked me for no reason! I was just minding my own business...

JAVERT: *(to FANTINE)* Your class of women is consigned by our laws entirely to the discretion of the police.

FANTINE: Yes, sir.

JAVERT: I have discretionary power as to what will become of you. As you all know, I am judge. I will condemn. Justice will be done! *(looks upon FANTINE with disgust)*

FANTINE: Yes, sir.

JAVERT: It is evident there has been a crime. Clearly a prostitute—or whatever you are—has made an attempt on the life of a citizen.

BAMATABOIS: Exactly!

JAVERT: You attacked and insulted a person of society. *(to an OFFICER)* Take this creature to jail. *(Then, turning to FANTINE)* You are to have six months of it.

FANTINE: Six months! Six months of prison! But... what will become of my daughter? My Cosette! I still owe the Thénardiers... *(She drags herself across the ground without rising, with clasped hands, and taking great strides on her knees.)* Monsieur Javert, I beseech your mercy. I assure you that I was not in the wrong. If you had seen the beginning. I swear to you by the good God that I was not to blame! That gentleman put snow down my back.

BAMATABOIS: *(sheepishly)* Well, I don't know what she is talking about.

FANTINE: Has anyone the right to put snow down our backs when we are walking along peaceably? I was doing no harm. *(coughs)* I am rather ill, as you see. He told me, I am ugly! I have no teeth! I know well that I have no longer those teeth. I didn't react, I said nothing; I said to myself, "The gentleman is amusing himself, do not speak to him." Yet he put the snow down my back. There must be a person here who saw it and can tell you that this is quite true? *(turns to ONLOOKERS)* Please. *(turns to JAVERT)* Please, Inspector, perhaps I did wrong to get angry, but when someone puts something cold down your back when you are not expecting it!

BAMATABOIS: Look at my hat! I think it's ruined.

FANTINE: I did wrong to spoil that gentleman's hat. Please sir, pardon me. Do me the favor today, for this once, Monsieur Javert. Hold! Please don't put me in prison! You see, there is a little girl who will be turned out into the street in the very heart of the winter; please have pity on me, Monsieur Javert!

> *At that moment FANTINE has become beautiful once more. From time to time, she pauses and tenderly kisses the police agent's coat. She would have softened a heart of granite; but a heart of wood cannot be softened.*

JAVERT: *(after a pause)* Have you entirely finished? You will get six months. Now march! The Eternal Father in person could do nothing more.

FANTINE: *(sinks down)* Please Lord, is there no Mercy?!

> *JAVERT turns his back. The SOLDIERS seize her by the arms. A few moments earlier JEAN VALJEAN has entered, but no one has paid any heed to him. He listens to FANTINE's despairing supplications. At the instant when the SOLDIERS lay their hands upon FANTINE, who will not rise, JEAN VALJEAN emerges from the shadow...*

JEAN VALJEAN: One moment, Inspector, if you please.

> *JAVERT raises his eyes and recognizes JEAN VALJEAN. He removes his hat and salutes him with a sort of aggrieved awkwardness.*

JAVERT: Mr. Mayor?

> *The words "Mr. Mayor" produce a curious effect upon FANTINE. She rises to her feet with one bound, thrusts aside the SOLDIERS with both arms, walks straight up to JEAN VALJEAN before anyone can prevent her, and gazing intently at him, with a bewildered air, cries.*

FANTINE: Ah! So it is you who are Monsieur le Maire! *(scoffs and spits in his face)*

JEAN VALJEAN: *(wiping face)* Inspector Javert, set this woman at liberty.

JAVERT: What? Are you mad?

FANTINE: *(delirious)* At liberty?! I am to be allowed to go?! No prison! Did I hear that right? It cannot have been that monster of a mayor! Was it you, my good

Monsieur Javert, who said that I was to be set free? Was it you? *(to BYSTANDERS)*

BYSTANDER: Not me.

BYSTANDER: Not me… it was Monsieur Mayor…

FANTINE: That monster of a mayor! He is the cause!? Just imagine… *(goes to WORKERS)* All because of a pack of rascally women, who gossip in the workroom. If that is not a horror, what is? To dismiss a poor girl *(to M. VICTURNIEN)* who is doing her work honestly! I can no longer earn enough for my poor Cosette. Look at me *(to JEAN VALJEAN)* … this misery is your fault!

JEAN VALJEAN: How much did you say that you owed?

FANTINE: *(continues, addressing the SOLDIERS)* Say, you fellows, did you see how I spit in his face? Ah! *(to JEAN VALJEAN)* You old wretch of a mayor, you came here to frighten me, didn't you? But I'm not afraid of you. I am afraid of Monsieur Javert. *(to JAVERT)*

JAVERT: As you should be.

FANTINE: Citizens of this town? I guess I am here for you all to amuse yourselves with! But you see, I cried because it hurt me. I was not expecting the ice, the cold… from the gentleman at all; I am not well; I have a cough; I seem to have a burning ball in my stomach. Marguerite tells me, 'Take care of yourself. Rest.' Here, feel, give me your hand; don't be afraid—it is here.

> *She no longer weeps; she places JAVERT'S coarse hand on her delicate, white throat and looks smilingly at him.*

JAVERT: Stop. You are a crazy woman. *(SOLDIERS grab FANTINE)* Mr. Mayor, you don't have any authority. I am the dispenser of justice. This pathetic woman has insulted a citizen.

JEAN VALJEAN: Inspector Javert, *(in a calm and conciliating tone)* if you would please listen. I believe you are an honest man. Here is the true state of the case: I was passing through the square just as you were uncovering the situation; I too made inquiries and did due diligence to learn everything of the matter; it was the townsman who was in the wrong and should be arrested.

BAMATABOIS: I beg your pardon!?

JAVERT: This wretch is an insult to society; she just insulted you.

JEAN VALJEAN: That concerns me. My own insult belongs to me. I can do what I please about it.

JAVERT: I beg Monsieur le Maire's pardon. The law—

JEAN VALJEAN: Inspector Javert, the highest law is conscience. I have heard this woman; I know what I am doing.

JAVERT: And I, Mr. Mayor, do not know what I see? I am not content.

JEAN VALJEAN: Then content yourself with obeying.

JAVERT: I am obeying my duty. My duty demands that this woman shall see her justice in prison… for six months.

JEAN VALJEAN: *(gently)* Heed this well; she will not serve a single day.

JAVERT: *(still respectful)* I am sorry to oppose Monsieur le Maire; it is for the first time in my life, but he will permit me to remark that I am within the bounds of my authority. This woman flung herself on Monsieur Bamatabois, who is an elector and the proprietor of that handsome house.

BAMATABOIS: I do own a very nice house.

JAVERT: In any case, Monsieur le Maire, this is a question of police regulations in the streets, and this concerns me. Detain this woman, Fantine.

JEAN VALJEAN: Enough. The matter to which you refer is one connected with the municipal police. According to the terms of articles nine, eleven, fifteen, and sixty-six of the code of criminal examination, I am the judge. I order that this woman shall be set at liberty.

BAMATABOIS: I think I will take my broken hat and be off.

JAVERT: But Mr. Mayor—

JEAN VALJEAN: I refer you to article eighty-one of the law of the 13th of December 1799, in regard to arbitrary detention.

JAVERT: Monsieur le Maire, permit me—

JEAN VALJEAN: Not another word.

JAVERT: But—

JEAN VALJEAN: You are dismissed.

> *JAVERT receives the blow erect, full in the face, in his breast, like a Russian soldier. He bows to the very earth before the mayor and exits. CROWD*

exits. FANTINE watches JAVERT go. Drops to her knees.

FANTINE: I have seen two men who held in their hands my liberty, my life, my soul, my child, in combat before my very eyes; one of these men was drawing me towards darkness, the other was leading me back towards the light. The angel has conquered the demon. Please forgive me.

JEAN VALJEAN: Forgive you? Forgive me! I knew nothing about what you have mentioned. I was ignorant of the fact that you had left my shop. Why did you not apply to me? But here—I will pay your debts. I will send for your child...

FANTINE: *(softly)* Cosette?

JEAN VALJEAN: ...or you shall go to her. I'll take care of you and your child. You shall not work any longer. You need rest. I will give you everything you may need. And listen! I declare to you that if all is as you say—and I do not doubt it—you have never ceased to be virtuous and holy in the sight of God. Oh, poor woman.

FANTINE: To have Cosette?! To leave this life of affliction... To live free, happy, respectable; to see all these realities of paradise blossom in the midst of my suffering and despair. Oh! Oh, my Cosette.

FANTINE'S limbs give way beneath her, she kneels in front of JEAN VALJEAN, and before he can prevent her she grasps his hand and presses her lips to it. Then she faints in his arms.

SCENE 9 ~ Mayor Madeleine's Home

Split scene, one at the THÉNARDIERS, the other at JEAN VALJEAN'S...

[THÉNARDIER'S INN...]

THÉNARDIER: *(opens a letter, money inside)* Well, would you look at that? Some ninny has taken a fancy to Fantine. She's sick. Get this: *(mocking)* Cosette's sick mother requires her presence.

BOTH: Awe...

THÉNARDIER: Ooo-la-ti-da!

MADAME THÉNARDIER: *(takes money)* I told you she would make us a fortune. Imagine what I can buy with this!

THÉNARDIER: Oh, no, my dear. Let's not allow the child to go. *(takes back the money)* That little lark, Collette, is going to turn into a milch cow.

[JEAN VALJEAN'S HOUSE...]

JEAN VALJEAN had FANTINE brought to his own house. He confided her to the sisters, who put her to bed. SISTER SIMPLICITY tends to her.

SISTER SIMPLICITY: There, there.

FANTINE: I have been a sinner; but when I have my child beside me, it will be a sign that God has pardoned me. While I was leading a bad life, I should not have liked to have my Cosette with me; I could not have borne her sad, astonished eyes.

SISTER SIMPLICITY: Just rest. Rest, my child.

FANTINE: It was for her sake that I did evil. I shall feel the benediction of the good God when Cosette is here. Right?! It will do me good to see that innocent creature. She is an angel, you see. At that age, the wings have not yet fallen off. *(falls asleep)*

JEAN VALJEAN enters.

JEAN VALJEAN: How is she?

SISTER SIMPLICITY: A burning fever comes and goes. She spent part of the night in delirium and raving… she rests now…

JEAN VALJEAN goes to her. Watches her. FANTINE awakes. She sees JEAN VALJEAN standing there. His gaze was full of pity, anguish, and supplication. He was absorbed in prayer. She gazed at him for a long time without daring to interrupt him. At last, she said timidly:

FANTINE: What… what are you doing?

JEAN VALJEAN: *(takes her hand, feels her pulse)* Shhh—I was praying to the martyr there on high. How do you feel?

FANTINE: I think that I am better. It is nothing.

JEAN VALJEAN: You have suffered much, poor mother. Rest now.

FANTINE: Cosette? Is she here?

JEAN VALJEAN: Soon… Tomorrow, perhaps. She may arrive at any moment.

FANTINE: Oh! How happy I will be! Why do the Thénardiers keep her so… she's my daughter… I need her, she will give me strength… *(cough, cough)*

SISTER SIMPLICITY: There, there. Yes, but first you need your rest… *(to JEAN VALJEAN)* You must make haste and get the child here.

JEAN VALJEAN: I shall send someone to fetch Cosette! If necessary, I will go myself.

[THÉNARDIER'S INN…]

THÉNARDIER: *(reads a letter)* Another letter! Man, these people are persistent.

MADAME THÉNARDIER: How will we respond?

THÉNARDIER: *(coming up with ideas)* Cosette is not quite well enough to take a journey in the winter? *(mocking)* She's far too delicate!

MADAME THÉNARDIER: We used that one.

THÉNARDIER: Pressing debts in the neighborhood?

MADAME THÉNARDIER: That too… I'll come up with something, I always do!

    BOTH laugh off.

[JEAN VALJEAN'S HOUSE…]

JEAN VALJEAN is pacing, somewhat agitated. SERVANT enters…

JACQUE: Excuse me, Father Madeleine...?

JEAN VALJEAN: Well! What is it? Forgive me.

JACQUE: Inspector Javert is here to see you.

JEAN VALJEAN: *(sighs)* Very well. *(exits FANTINE'S room)* Hello, Inspector Javert. What can I do for you?

JAVERT: Mr. Mayor, a culpable act has been committed.

JEAN VALJEAN: What act?

JAVERT: An inferior agent of the authorities has failed in respect, and in the gravest manner, towards a magistrate. I have come to bring the fact to your knowledge, as it is my duty to do.

JEAN VALJEAN: Who is the agent?

JAVERT: I.

JEAN VALJEAN: You?

JAVERT: I.

JEAN VALJEAN: And who is the magistrate who has reason to complain of the agent?

JAVERT: You, Mr. Mayor. *(eyes still cast down)* Mr. Mayor, I have come to request you to instigate the authorities to dismiss me. *(JEAN VALJEAN opened his mouth in amazement. JAVERT interrupts)* You will say that I might have handed in my resignation, but that does not suffice. Handing in one's resignation is honorable. I have failed in my duty; I ought to be punished; I must be turned out.

JEAN VALJEAN: Come, now! Why? What nonsense is this? What culpable act have you done to me? I do not understand.

JAVERT: Mr. Mayor, weeks ago, in consequence of the scene over that woman, I was furious, and I informed against you.

JEAN VALJEAN: Informed against me?!

JAVERT: I believed you were an ex-convict.

JEAN VALJEAN: A convict?

JAVERT: I thought it was so. I had had the idea for a long time; a resemblance; your strength; the adventure with old Fauchelevent ...

JEAN VALJEAN: Absurd!

JAVERT: I took you for a certain Jean Valjean. He was a convict whom I saw at Toulon. After leaving the galleys, this Jean Valjean, as it appears, robbed a bishop, as well as a little Savoyard. Then he disappeared. I believed you were him and I turned you in—yet the real Jean Valjean has been found.

JEAN VALJEAN: *(questioning)* Oh?

JAVERT: This is the way it is, Mr. Mayor. It seems that there was an old fellow, wretched creature, who was called Father Champmathieu. No one paid any attention to him. Nevertheless, he was arrested for the theft of some cider apples from—well, no matter. The scamp is locked up. Up to this point, it was merely an affair of a misdemeanor. But here is where Providence intervened. While in prison there is an ex-convict named Brevet, who is detained for I know not what, and who has been appointed turnkey of the house because of good behavior. Mr. Mayor, no sooner had Champmathieu arrived than…

[POP OUT SCENE…]

BREVET: *(offstage, exclaiming)* Eh! Why, I know that man! Take a good look at me, my good man! You are Jean Valjean! Ah—yes, Jean Valjean!

CHAMPMATHIEU: *(astonished)* I do not know what you are talking about? Who's Valjean?

BREVET: Don't play the innocent dodge. You are Jean Valjean! You have been in the galleys of Toulon; it was twenty years ago; we were there together.

CHAMPMATHIEU: Me? No…

[JEAN VALJEAN'S HOUSE…]

JAVERT: Champmathieu denies it. Parbleu! You understand. When such people are not mud, they are dust.

JEAN VALJEAN: I see…

JAVERT: Inquiries were made at Toulon. Besides Brevet, there are only two convicts in existence who have seen Jean Valjean; they are Cochepaille and Chenildieu and are sentenced for life.

JEAN VALJEAN: And they have identified him as Valjean?

JAVERT: Oh yes, and these convicts will receive special considerations for their testimony… reduced time. It is the galleys for life for Valjean; the old scamp has been found and will be condemned.

JEAN VALJEAN: In truth, all these details interest me but little. There is other work at hand…

JAVERT: No sir, why, I thought that I had said to Monsieur le Maire that the case is being tried to-morrow, and that I am to set out by diligence to-night. I shall go there to give my testimony. I have been summoned.

JEAN VALJEAN: That is well. (*Dismisses JAVERT with a wave of the hand. JAVERT does not withdraw.*)

JAVERT: Excuse me, Mr. Mayor.

JEAN VALJEAN: What is it now?

JAVERT: Mr. Mayor, there is still something of which I must remind you.

JEAN VALJEAN: What is it?

JAVERT: That I must be dismissed.

JEAN VALJEAN: Javert, you are a man of honor. You exaggerate your fault. Moreover, this is an offence which concerns me. You deserve a promotion instead of degradation. I wish you to retain your post.

JAVERT: Mr. Mayor, I cannot grant you that. I have suspected you unjustly.

JEAN VALJEAN: It is your right to cherish suspicion…

JAVERT: Suspicions directed above ourselves is an abuse. But without proofs, in a fit of rage, with the object of wreaking my vengeance? I have denounced you as a convict—you, a respectable man! If one of my subordinates had done what I have done, I should have declared him unworthy of the service and have expelled him.

JEAN VALJEAN: Well…

JAVERT: *(continues)* I have often been severe in the course of my life towards others. I am a man of justice. That is just. Now, if I were not severe towards myself, all the justice that I have done would become injustice. Ought I to spare myself more than others?

JEAN VALJEAN: No?

JAVERT: I should be good for nothing but to chastise others, and not myself! I do not desire that you should treat me kindly. Come! If you had been what I thought you, I should not have been kind to you, not I! I simply require you to discharge me. I have misused the police. I am no more than a police spy. Mr. Mayor, I shall continue to serve until I am superseded. And with that I say, good day, sir. *(bows and leaves)*

JEAN VALJEAN: *(quietly, in thought)* Good day…

> *JEAN VALJEAN notices the candlesticks… and a box. The box contains the coin from Gervais.*

JEAN VALJEAN: These must be destroyed… *(goes to them like he's going to put them into the fire… BISHOP appears)* My dear Bishop… it's you. I am a different man, am I not? What you wanted from me; did I not carry it out? Yet, I now want to run. Do I give myself up? If I take Champmathieu's place, that means prison for me. What will become of Fantine, or Cosette? What about my workers - is not my factory a home for them? Do I look down or up, or the other way?

BISHOP: You are not your past, but your choice. A soul is not judged by what it fears—but by what it does for love. You may only be a small light, my son—but in great darkness, even the smallest light can shine. Do what is right… even if it breaks your heart. Of all things the human heart is the one that sheds the most light.

JEAN VALJEAN: Who am I? You taught me, I'm not in this world to take care of my life. I'm here to care for others. I will pick up my shield.

ACT 2

SCENE 1 ~ Courthouse

The PRESIDENT sits center, next to ASSISTANTS.
CHAMPMATHIEU, in shackles, stands between
TWO SOLDIERS. He is at least sixty, with
something indescribably coarse, stupid, and
frightened about him. BAMATOBOIS sits in the
Jury Box. BREVET, COCHEPAILLE, and
CHENILDIEU are waiting to testify. No one seems
to notice JEAN VALJEAN entering at some point...

COURT OFFICIAL: We have in our grasp not only a
marauder, a stealer of fruit; we have here, in our hands, a
bandit, an old offender who has broken his ban, an ex-
convict of the most dangerous description, a malefactor
named Jean Valjean.

COURTROOM OBSERVERS: *(murmurs)*

CHAMPMATHIEU: *(pleading)* The name's
Champmathieu... please I tell you. I am not Valjean!?

PRESIDENT: Silence. Read on...

COURT OFFICIAL: Justice has long been in search of
this man. Eight years ago, upon emerging from the
galleys at Toulon, he stole from our dear Bishop of
Digne, he committed a highway robbery, accompanied
by violence, on the person of a mere child, a Savoyard
named Little Gervais; a crime provided for by article 383
of the Penal Code.

81

CHAMPMATHIEU: I did no such thing… I'm innocent. Innocent, I say…

COURTROOM OBSERVERS: *(murmurs)*

PRESIDENT: *(to CHAMPMATHIEU, in a severe voice)* Prisoner, pay attention. Your embarrassment condemns you.

PROSECUTOR: It is evident that your name is not Champmathieu.

PRESIDENT: Can we establish he is the convict, Jean Valjean?

PROSECUTOR: Of course, your honor.

CHAMPMATHIEU: You are very wicked; that you are! I have stolen nothing. I am a man who does not have something to eat every day…

PRESIDENT: Enough!

PROSECUTOR: It is evident that you have been guilty of entering, and of the theft of ripe apples from the Pierron orchard. The gentlemen of the jury will form their own opinion.

CHAMPMATHIEU: I have stolen nothing. I found a broken branch with apples on the ground; I picked up the branch without knowing that it would get me into trouble. I don't know how to explain; I have no education; I am a poor man; I have not stolen; I picked up from the ground things that were lying there. You say, Jean Valjean? I don't know this person; my name is Champmathieu. Why is everybody pursuing me so furiously?

SOLDIERS react to hush CHAMPMATHIEU.

PROSECUTOR: Gentlemen, in the absence of Inspector Javert, I think it my duty to remind you of what he said here a few hours ago. As you may or may not know, Inspector Javert is an estimable man. He does honor by his rigorous and strict probity to inferior but important functions. This was his deposition

---

[FREEZE. JAVERT POPS OUT, walking around CHAMPMATHIEU in arrogance...]

JAVERT: I do not even stand in need of circumstantial proofs and moral presumptions to give the lie to the prisoner's denial. I recognize him perfectly. The name of this man is not Champmathieu; he is an ex-convict named Jean Valjean. He is vicious and much to be feared. It is only with extreme regret that he was released at the expiration of his term. He underwent nineteen years of penal servitude for theft. He made five or six attempts to escape. Besides the theft from Little Gervais and from the Pierron orchard, I suspect him of a theft committed in the house of His Grace the late Bishop of Digne. I often saw him at the time when I was adjutant of the galley-guard at the prison in Toulon. I repeat that I recognize him perfectly.

JAVERT walks out backwards... exits.

[UNFREEZE...]

COURTROOM OBSERVERS: *(murmurs...)*

PRESIDENT: Silence! We should hear the three witnesses: Brevet, Chenildieu, and Cochepaille…

> *The audience in suspense; all breasts heaved as though they had contained but one soul. The ex-convict BREVET, a man of sixty with a businessman's face and the air of a rascal, steps forward.*

PROSECUTOR: *(acknowledges)* Brevet. Tell us what you know. *(Turns towards CHAMPMATHIEU)* Rise, prisoner.

BREVET: *(pathetic, yet proud)* I had become something in the nature of a turnkey. You see? I tries to make myself use.

PROSECUTOR: Brevet, take a good look at the accused, recall and tell us on your soul and conscience, if you persist in recognizing this man as your former companion in the galleys, Jean Valjean?

> *BREVET looks at the prisoner, then turns towards the court.*

BREVET: Yes, Mr. President, I was the first to recognize him, and I stick to it; that man is Jean Valjean, who entered at Toulon in 1796, and left in 1815. I left a year later. He was sly at the galleys: I recognize him positively.

PROSECUTOR: Take your seat. *(to BREVET)* Prisoner, *(to CHAMPMATHIEU)* remain standing. Chenildieu, prisoner for life, you are serving out your sentence at the galleys of Toulon?

CHENILDIEU: Aye…

PROSECUTOR: Do you recognize this man?

CHENILDIEU: *(burst out laughing)* Pardieu, as if I didn't recognize him?! We were attached to the same chain for five years.

PROSECUTOR: Take your seat. Finally, Cochepaille, do you recognize the man who is standing before you?

COCHEPAILLE: He is Jean Valjean. He was even called Jean-the-Screw, because he was so strong.

COURTROOM OBSERVERS: *(murmurs…)*

PROSECUTOR: Each of these affirmations from these three men, evidently sincere and in good faith, clearly indicate that this man is none other than…

JEAN VALJEAN: NOT Jean Valjean…

COURTROOM OBSERVERS: Who… what? *(murmurs…)*

PRESIDENT: Who said that?

JEAN VALJEAN: I did.

COURTROOM OBSERVERS: *(murmurs…)*

JEAN VALJEAN: *(walks toward them)* Brevet! Chenildieu! Cochepaille! Look here!

COURTROOM OBSERVERS: M. Madeleine, what is he doing here?!

JEAN VALJEAN: Do you not recognize me?

All three remain speechless and indicate by a shake of the head that they do not know him.
COCHEPAILLE, intimidated, makes a military salute.

JEAN VALJEAN: *(turns to the jury and court, speaking gently)* Gentlemen of the jury, please, I beg you, order the prisoner to be released! Mr. President, have me arrested. This man is not the man whom you are in search of; it is I: I am Jean Valjean.

> *Not a mouth breathes. The first commotion of astonishment gives way to a silence like that of the grave. The PRESIDENT's face reflects sympathy and sadness. He exchanges a rapid sign with the PROSECUTOR and speaks a few low-toned words to the ASSISTANT JUDGES.*

PRESIDENT: Gentlemen of the jury, you all know, by reputation at least, the honorable Mayor Madeleine; if there is a physician in the audience, we request you to attend to the mayor, and to conduct him to his home.

JEAN VALJEAN: I thank you, Mr. District-Attorney, but I am not mad; you shall see; you were on the point of committing a great error; release this man! I am fulfilling a duty; I am that miserable criminal.

COURTROOM OBSERVERS: What! Nonsense? What did he say?

JEAN VALJEAN: I am the only one here who sees the matter clearly, and I am telling you the truth. God, who is on high, looks down on what I am doing at this moment, and that suffices. You can take me, for here I am but I have done my best; I concealed myself under another name; I have become rich; I have become a mayor.

FAUCHELEVENT: He saved my life!

JEAN VALJEAN: I have tried to re-enter the ranks of the honest. I will not narrate the whole story of my life to you; but I did rob the forgiving Bishop, and it is true; it is true that I robbed Little Gervais; they were right in telling you that Jean Valjean was a very vicious wretch. Perhaps it was not altogether his fault. Listen, honorable judges! A man who has been so greatly humbled as I have has neither any remonstrances to make to Providence, nor any advice to give to society; but, you see, the infamy from which I have tried to escape is an injurious thing; the galleys make the convict what he is; reflect upon that, if you please. Before going to the galleys, I was a poor peasant, with very little intelligence, a sort of idiot; the galleys wrought a change in me. I was stupid; I became vicious: I was a block of wood; I became a firebrand. Later on, through indulgence and kindness, a light began to shine on me.

PROSECUTOR: What are you saying?

JEAN VALJEAN: You will find at my house, in a box on the mantel, the forty-sou piece which I stole, seven years ago, from Little Gervais. Do not condemn this man! If Javert were here, he would recognize me. *(He turns to the three convicts.)* Well, I recognize you; do you remember, Brevet? Do you remember the knitted suspenders with a checked pattern which you wore in the galleys?

BREVET: (*surprised, surveying him from head to foot*) I… I do.

JEAN VALJEAN: Chenildieu, you who conferred on yourself the name of 'Jenie-Dieu,' your whole right shoulder bears a deep burn, because you one day laid your shoulder against the chafing-dish full of coals, in order to efface the three letters T. F. P., which are still visible, nevertheless; answer, is this true?

CHENILDIEU: It is true.

JEAN VALJEAN: Cochepaille, you have, near the bend in your left arm, a date stamped in blue letters with burnt powder; the date is that of the landing of the Emperor at Cannes, March 1, 1815; pull up your sleeve!

> *COCHEPAILLE pushes up his sleeve; all eyes are focused on him and on his bare arm. The unhappy man turns to the spectators and the judges with a smile that rends the hearts of all who saw it. It is a smile of triumph; it is also a smile of despair.*

JEAN VALJEAN: As you can see plainly, I am Jean Valjean.

COURTROOM OBSERVERS: He is. Oh my. *(murmurs…)*

JEAN VALJEAN: I do not wish to disturb the court further. I shall withdraw, since you do not arrest me. I have many things to do. The district-attorney knows who I am; he knows where I reside; he can have me arrested when he likes.

> *JEAN VALJEAN exits.*

CHAMPMATHIEU: Does that mean I am free? I am free…

> *WORKERS pass through as the courthouse scene exits.*

WORKER 1: Did you hear the news?

WORKER 2: I heard he left the factory to us!? What's to become of the hospital?

WORKER 3: The whole town is abuzz.

WORKER 4: How can a saint be an ex-convict?

MADAME VICTURNIEN: Ladies, ladies, get to work, you don't want to be late!

Finishes watching them pass. FAUCHELEVENT enters…

MADAME VICTURNIEN: Father Fauchelevent, have you heard the latest developments!? Your savior is a scoundrel!

FAUCHELEVENT: Madame Victurnien, the man saved my life. I will forever be indebted to him. Do you not remember how he gave to our community?

TOWNSPEOPLE enter…

MADAME VICTURNIEN: He's a disgrace to our town, that man!

TOWNSPERSON 1: He's brought shame to us all.

TOWNSPERSON 2: If someone asks if I know him, I will lie.

TOWNSPERSON 3: Do you know if he has been arrested yet?

TOWNSPERSON 4: If you ask me, they should lock him up and throw away the key!

TOWNSPERSON 5: How dare he try to fool us…

TOWNSPERSON 6: I never trusted him…

TOWNSPERSON 7: Good riddance!

FAUCHELEVENT: How quickly you forget what he did… for all of us.

SCENE 2 ~ Monsieur Mayor No More

SISTER SIMPLICITY tends to FANTINE, who is in and out of delirium. JEAN VALJEAN enters, deep in thought.

SISTER SIMPLICITY: Thank God, you are back. What is it? You look like you have seen a ghost?

JEAN VALJEAN: It's nothing. How is Fantine?

SISTER SIMPLICITY: Worse, I'm afraid. She may only have a little time left.

FANTINE murmurs deliriously...

JEAN VALJEAN: What is it, Fantine? I am back. Let me pray with you.

FANTINE: Did you have a pleasant trip, Monsieur le Maire? Oh! How good you were to go and get Cosette for me! Alas! She must have forgotten me by this time, poor darling! Children have no memories. They are like birds. A child sees one thing to-day and another thing to-morrow. Oh! If you only knew how I have suffered, putting such questions as that to myself during all the time of my wretchedness.

JEAN VALJEAN: There, there, it is all past.

FANTINE: I am happy. Oh, how I should like to see her! Do you think her pretty, Monsieur le Maire? Is not my daughter beautiful? Could she not be brought for just one little instant? She might be taken away directly afterwards. Tell me; you are the master; it could be so if you chose!

JEAN VALJEAN: *(takes her hand)* Cosette is beautiful, she is well. You shall see her soon; but calm yourself; soon you will be happy.

FANTINE: How happy we are going to be! We shall have a little garden the very first thing. *(to SISTER SIMPLICITY)* Monsieur Madeleine has promised it to me.

SISTER SIMPLICITY: Yes, of course.

FANTINE: My daughter will play in the garden. She will run over the grass after butterflies. I will watch her. You will watch over her, say it is so, Father Madeleine.

JEAN VALJEAN: Yes, my dear.

FANTINE: You will protect her?

JEAN VALJEAN: Like my own.

JAVERT enters cautiously...

FANTINE: She must know her letters by this time. I will make her spell. We will tell each other stories. *(shrieks in anguish, seeing JAVERT)* Monsieur Madeleine, save me!

JEAN VALJEAN: *(turns, notices JAVERT)* Fantine, *(in the gentlest and calmest of voices)* be at ease; it is not for you that he is come.

SISTER SIMPLICITY: Calm yourself dear, you must stay calm.

JEAN VALJEAN: *(to JAVERT)* I know what you want.

JAVERT: *(roared)* Be quick about it! *(advances to the middle of the room)* See here now! Art thou coming?

JAVERT seizes JEAN VALJEAN by the collar. FANTINE sees the mayor bow his head. It seems to her the world is ending.

FANTINE: *(shrieks)* Monsieur le Maire!

JAVERT: *(bursts out laughing)* There is no longer any Monsieur le Maire here!

SISTER SIMPLICITY: Please Monsieur, you are disturbing the lady.

JEAN VALJEAN: Javert—

JAVERT: Call me Mr. Inspector.

JEAN VALJEAN: Monsieur, I should like to say a word to you in private.

JAVERT: Aloud! Say it aloud! People are in the habit of talking aloud to me.

FANTINE grows agitated.

JEAN VALJEAN: *(in a lower tone)* I have a request to make of you—

JAVERT: What difference does that make to me? I shall not listen.

JEAN VALJEAN: *(turns to him quickly, voice low and rapid)* Please sir, if you would just grant me three days' grace! Three days in which to go and fetch her child. I will pay whatever is necessary. You shall accompany me if you choose.

JAVERT: You are making sport of me! Come now, I did not think you such a fool! You ask me to give you three days in which to run away! You say that it is for the purpose of fetching that creature's child! Ah! Ah! That's good! That's really good.

FANTINE: *(seized with a fit of trembling)* My child!? Please go and fetch my child! She is not here, then! Answer me, sister, where is Cosette? I want my child! Monsieur le Maire!

SISTER SIMPLICITY: Calm yourself, dear.

JAVERT: *(stamps his foot)* Hold your tongue, you wretch! It's a pretty sort of a place where convicts are magistrates, and where women of the town are cared for like countesses! Ah! But we are going to change all that; it is high time! *(stares at FANTINE, grasping JEAN VALJEAN)* I tell you, mademoiselle— *(mocking)* —that there is no Monsieur le Maire here, only a thief, a brigand, a convict named Jean Valjean! And I have him in my grasp!

> *FANTINE raises herself in bed with a bound, supporting herself on stiffened arms. She gazes at JEAN VALJEAN, then at JAVERT, then at the nun. Her mouth opens as if to speak; a rattle emerges from her throat, her teeth chatter; she stretches out her arms, convulsively fumbling, then suddenly falls back on her pillow.*

SISTER SIMPLICITY: *(approaching)* She is gone. A death that signifies entrance into the great light.

JEAN VALJEAN: You have murdered her.

JAVERT: Let's have an end of this! I am not here to listen to argument. The guard is below; march on, or you'll get the thumbscrews!

JEAN VALJEAN grabs the fire poker.

JEAN VALJEAN: Inspector Javert, you are law without feeling. You only seek blind justice. I advise you not to disturb me at this moment.

> *JAVERT trembles yet does not call for the guard. JEAN VALJEAN bends toward FANTINE and speaks to her in a low voice. What did he say? No one hears. He gently lifts her head, arranges it on the pillow like a mother would for her child, and closes her eyes. FANTINE's face is strangely illuminated. Her hand hangs off the bed. JEAN VALJEAN kneels, lifts her hand, and kisses it. Then he stands and turns to JAVERT.*

JEAN VALJEAN: Now, I am at your disposal. Lead on…

JAVERT: No, I insist. (*Motions for him to move. JEAN VALJEAN exits. Offstage, a tussle is heard…*) Guard! Don't just stand there… seize the beast!

GUARD 1: *(offstage)* He can't have gone far…

GUARD 2: *(offstage)* I saw him head down the alley…

JAVERT: Idiots! I'll get you, Jean Valjean! This is not over!

> *Back on stage…*

SISTER SIMPLICITY: *(covering FANTINE)* He is a good man, he is. He will find and protect your daughter. My God, who art in heaven…

> *JEAN VALJEAN enters again, through the window.*

JEAN VALJEAN: Sister Simplicity, quickly… retrieve the gardener's coat from the hall closet.

> *SISTER SIMPLICITY exits and returns. JEAN VALJEAN pulls one of his old shirts from a cupboard, tearing it into strips. He wraps the BISHOP'S silver candlesticks in the linen. He moves without haste or agitation. Then, he opens a small box on the mantle and removes the forty-sou piece stolen from Little Gervais.*

JEAN VALJEAN: This is the forty sou I took from the Savoyard so many years ago. *(takes a piece of paper and writes a note)* Give this to the priest, pay my expenses, and give everything to the poor. Monsieur le Maire is no more.

SCENE 3 ~ The Thénardier's Inn and The Well

COSETTE sits in her usual place beneath the table near the chimney—her kennel. She is in rags; her bare feet are thrust into wooden shoes. By the firelight, she knits woolen stockings. Laughter and chatter come from two fresh young voices— ÉPONINE and AZELMA. The inn is alive with patrons. The THÉNARDIERS tend to their guests.

GIRLS: (*Chanting a hand game, giggling*)

MADAME THÉNARDIER: Girls, girls, stop being silly.

GAVROCHE: (*offstage*) Mom-ma… mom-ma… MOMMA!!

THÉNARDIER: Your son is squalling. Do go and see what he wants, already. He's scaring our guests.

MADAME THÉNARDIER: Bah! He bothers me.

COSETTE is rarely still. When not under the table, she runs up and down stairs, washes, sweeps, dusts, pants, and hauls heavy items—all without mercy. A fierce mistress and a venomous master. The Thénardier hostelry is a spider's web, and COSETTE its trembling captive.

INN MAN 1: Excuuuuuse me… my horse has not been watered.

MADAME THÉNARDIER: Yes, it has.

INN MAN 1: I tell you that it has not.

COSETTE emerges from under the table. AZELMA and ÉPONINE listen in.

COSETTE: Oh yes, sir! The horse has had a drink. He drank out of a bucket—a whole bucketful—and it was I who took the water to him… and I spoke to him.

AZELMA: Who does Cosette think she's fooling??

ÉPONINE: She doesn't want to go to the well. You know she's afraid.

INN MAN 1: *(loudly, for the other patrons to hear)* There's a brat in here as big as my fist, there is! She tells lies as big as the house.

COSETTE creeps back under the table.

INN MAN 1: I tell you he has not been watered, you little jade! He has a way of blowing when he's had no water—I know it well.

MADAME THÉNARDIER: Oh well, sir… if you say the beast has not been watered, it must be. *(glances around)* Well, now! Where's that other beast?

She bends down and discovers COSETTE in her kennel. Then yells and hands her the bucket.

MADAME THÉNARDIER: Are you coming? Go and water that horse!

COSETTE: *(feebly)* But, Madame, there is no water.

MADAME THÉNARDIER: Well, go and get some, then!

THÉNARDIER: Help these days…

COSETTE drops her head and goes for the empty bucket near the chimney, passing AZELMA and ÉPONINE.

AZELMA: I hear the beasts are out tonight… walking on the grass. Perhaps you'll see spectres moving in the trees?

ÉPONINE: It's pitch black out there tonight. No one walks alone in the forest at night… without trembling.

MADAME THÉNARDIER: See here, Mam'selle Toad, on your way back, you will get a loaf of bread from the baker. Here's a fifteen-sou piece.

COSETTE takes the coin silently and places it in the pocket of her apron. She stands motionless, bucket in hand, staring at the open door as if hoping someone will rescue her.

MADAME THÉNARDIER: Get along with you!

COSETTE exits. A few INN PATRONS are outside.

INN PERSON 1: Where can that child be going?

INN PERSON 2: Is it a werewolf child? It's dreadfully dark out here tonight.

INN PERSON 3: Why—it's the Lark! The Thénardiers' servant girl. She's going to fetch water. The poor dear.

INN PERSON 1: All the way out there? That's seven or eight minutes' walk from the edge of the woods to the spring. On a dark night like this?

INN PERSON 2: She's liable to catch a cold.

INN PERSON 1: Speaking of cold… let's get back inside and warm ourselves up.

COSETTE walks with urgency. She keeps her eyes down, fearing what might lurk in the branches and shadows. At the spring, it is pitch dark. She feels around with her hand, plunges the bucket into the water, and does not notice the fifteen-sou piece falling into the spring. She draws out the bucket and sets it on the grass, exhausted. She sits, unable to move. A faint light begins to glow—a single star. JEAN VALJEAN enters behind her, unnoticed. He watches her quietly.

COSETTE: *(startled)* Oh—Would you look at that… a lone star. Is that you, mother? You startled me. I thought there was only darkness here tonight.

The light begins to fade.

COSETTE: No… dear star. Do not leave me. Do not! Please! Please… I will not cry, I will not cry. Madame Thénardier is always watching… pick up the bucket, Cosette… Please Lord, have mercy… help me.

BISHOP: The darkness—is it not bewildering? Man requires light. Whoever buries himself in the opposite of day feels his heart contract. When the eye sees black, the heart sees trouble. Will you be her light?

JEAN VALJEAN, still silent, steps forward and lifts the bucket. COSETTE is not afraid.

JEAN VALJEAN: My child, what you are carrying is very heavy for you.

COSETTE: *(raises her head)* Yes, sir.

JEAN VALJEAN: Give it to me, I will carry it for you. *(COSETTE releases the handle. He walks beside her.)* It really is very heavy. And have you come from far like this?

COSETTE: I come from town to the spring in the forest. It's a good quarter of an hour's walk from here.

JEAN VALJEAN: Your mother makes you fetch water at this late hour?

COSETTE: Other people have mothers. I have none.

JEAN VALJEAN stops. He sets the bucket down and gently places his hands on the child's shoulders, trying to see her face in the dark.

JEAN VALJEAN: What is your name, child?

COSETTE: Cosette.

JEAN VALJEAN: *(picks up the bucket and resumes walking)* Where do you live, little one?

COSETTE: In Montfermeil, with Madame Thénardier. She sent me to get the water. She is my mistress. She keeps the inn.

JEAN VALJEAN: The inn? Well, I am going to lodge there tonight. Is there no servant in Madame Thénardier's house?

COSETTE: I? I work.

JEAN VALJEAN: All day long?

COSETTE: Yes, sir. Sometimes, when I have finished my work, they let me play. Though Ponine and Zelma will not let me play with their dolls. I have only a little

101

lead sword, no longer than that. *(holds up her finger)* And it does not cut… *(stops, timidly touches his arm)* Monsieur?

JEAN VALJEAN: What, my child?

COSETTE: We are quite near… Will you let me take my bucket now? If Madame sees that someone has carried it for me, she will beat me.

> *JEAN VALJEAN hands her the bucket. An instant later, they are at the tavern door.*

MADAME THÉNARDIER: Ah! So it's you, you little wretch! You've certainly taken your time! You must have been amusing yourself!

COSETTE: Madame, here's a gentleman who wants a lodging.

> *MADAME THÉNARDIER speedily replaces her gruff air with an amiable grimace, a change of aspect common to tavern-keepers. She eagerly scans the newcomer.*

MADAME THÉNARDIER: This is the *(looks him over)* gentleman?

JEAN VALJEAN: Yes, Madame. (raises his hand to his hat)

> *Wealthy travelers are not so polite. This gesture, and an inspection of the stranger's costume and baggage, which the THÉNARDIERS take in with one glance.*

THÉNARDIER: *(dryly)* Enter, my good man.

MADAME THÉNARDIER: Ah! See here, my good man; I am very sorry, but I have no room left. *(pulls THÉNARDIER aside)* Let me handle this, you idiot husband.

JEAN VALJEAN: Put me where you like, in the attic, in the stable. I will pay as though I occupied a room.

MADAME THÉNARDIER: Forty sous.

JEAN VALJEAN: Forty sous; agreed. *(hands over the money)*

INN PERSON 4: *(in a low tone to MADAME THÉNARDIER)* Forty sous? Why, the charge is only twenty sous!

MADAME THÉNARDIER: Shhh! It is forty in his case. I don't lodge poor folks for less.

THÉNARDIER: That's true. It ruins a house to have such people in it.

In the meantime, JEAN VALJEAN, laying his bundle and his cudgel on a bench, seats himself at a table. COSETTE hastens to place a bottle of wine and a glass before him. The MERCHANT—MAN 1—who demanded the bucket, takes it to his horse himself. COSETTE resumes her place under the kitchen table, knitting. JEAN VALJEAN barely moistens his lips with the wine and watches her with peculiar attention.

MADAME THÉNARDIER: By the way, Cosette, where's that bread?

ÉPONINE: She has no bread? Do you think she ate it?

AZELMA: She better have a good excuse!

COSETTE: (*emerges with great haste from beneath the table*) Madame, the baker's shop was shut.

MADAME THÉNARDIER: You should have knocked.

COSETTE: I did knock, Madame. He did not open the door.

ÉPONINE: Ma-ma will find out tomorrow whether that is true.

AZELMA: And if she's telling a lie, she'll lead her a pretty dance.

MADAME THÉNARDIER: So… *(extends hand to COSETTE)* give me back my fifteen-sou piece, you little pig.

> *COSETTE plunges her hand into her apron pocket and turns green. The fifteen-sou piece is not there.*

MADAME THÉNARDIER: Ah, come now, did you hear me?

> *COSETTE turns her pocket inside out; there is nothing. She is petrified, speechless.*

MADAME THÉNARDIER: Have you lost that fifteen-sou piece, you idiot child? Or do you mean to rob me of it? Answer me swiftly… *(reaches for the cat-o'-nine-tails hanging on a nail in the chimney-corner)*

COSETTE: Mercy, Madame, Madame! I… I…!

JEAN VALJEAN: *(as MADAME THÉNARDIER is about to whip COSETTE, bends down as if picking* *something up)* Pardon me, Madame, but just now I caught sight of something which had fallen from this little one's apron pocket and rolled aside. Perhaps this is it. *(hands her a silver coin)*

MADAME THÉNARDIER: Yeeeeessss, that's it… *(to COSETTE in a lowered tone)* Don't let this ever happen again! *(points her to the kennel)*

THÉNARDIER: By the way, would you like some supper? My wife makes a taste(less)… um—tasty mutton soup.

> *MADAME THÉNARDIER goes and makes him a plate, though JEAN VALJEAN does not reply.*

INN PERSON 1: What sort of man is that?

INN PERSON 2: He's probably some frightfully poor wretch. He hasn't a sou to pay for a supper.

INN PERSON 1: Will he even pay for his lodging?

MADAME THÉNARDIER: It's very lucky, all the same, that it didn't occur to him to steal the money that was on the floor.

> *ÉPONINE and AZELMA begin to bicker over their dolls.*

ÉPONINE: It's my turn to play with her… give her to me.

ALZEMA: You're not the boss of me! I want to be the momma now.

MADAME THÉNARDIER: *(grumbling, yet full of adoration)* Ah! Children! *(smoothing their hair, tying their ribbons afresh, then releasing them gently)* What frights they are! Play nicely, or I will send you to bed like your nasty little brother, Gavroche.

> *The girls seat themselves in the chimney-corner, turning the doll over on their knees with joyous chatter. From time to time, COSETTE raises her eyes from her knitting and watches with a melancholy air. ÉPONINE and AZELMA do not look at her. She is as a dog to them.*
> *COSETTE is distracted and forgets her work. Her eyes linger on the little ones' play.*

MADAME THÉNARDIER: Courgette! Ah! I've caught you at it! So that's the way you work! I'll make you work to the tune of the whip—that I will.

JEAN VALJEAN: *(to himself, but heard)* Bah, let the poor girl play!

MADAME THÉNARDIER: She must work, since she eats. I don't feed her to do nothing.

JEAN VALJEAN: What is she making?

MADAME THÉNARDIER: Stockings, if you please. Stockings for my little girls, who have none, so to speak, and who are absolutely barefoot just now.

JEAN VALJEAN: When will she have finished this pair of stockings?

MADAME THÉNARDIER: She has at least three or four good days' work on them still, the lazy creature!

JEAN VALJEAN: And how much will that pair of stockings be worth when she has finished them?

MADAME THÉNARDIER: *(with a glance of disdain)* Thirty sous… at least.

JEAN VALJEAN: Will you sell them for five francs?

INN PERSON 3: Good heavens! Five francs! The deuce, I should think so!

THÉNARDIER: Yes, sir; if stockings are your fancy, you will be allowed to have that pair for five francs. We can refuse nothing to travelers.

MADAME THÉNARDIER: *(in her curt and peremptory fashion)* However, you must pay on the spot.

JEAN VALJEAN: *(drawing a five-franc piece from his pocket and laying it on the table)* Here. *(turns to COSETTE)* Now I own her work; play, my child.

INN PERSON 4: *(abandoning his glass and examining the coin)* But it's true! A real hind wheel! And not counterfeit!

INN PERSON 3: He pays for the child to play. How particular!

> *THÉNARDIER approaches and silently puts the coin in his pocket.*

COSETTE: Is it true, Madame? May I play?

MADAME THÉNARDIER: *(in a terrible voice)* Play!

COSETTE: Thanks, Madame. Thank you, Monsieur.

> *COSETTE begins to make a baby from a stick and her apron.*

AZELMA: Who can this man be?

ÉPONINE: *(AZELMA listens admiringly)* I think I have seen millionaires with coats like that before. But look at her. What is she going to play with? She has no doll.

> *Meanwhile, the INN PATRONS begin to sing a song, laughing until the ceiling shakes. THÉNARDIER encourages them. While ÉPONINE and AZELMA bundle their dolls, COSETTE dresses her sword like a doll, lays it in her arms, and sings softly to lull it to sleep. MADAME THÉNARDIER sets her elbows on JEAN VALJEAN'S table.*

MADAME THÉNARDIER: *(assuming a sweetish air)* Monsieur. You see, sir, I am willing that the child should play; I do not oppose it. But it is good for once—because you are generous. You see, she has nothing. She must needs work.

JEAN VALJEAN: Then this child is not yours?

MADAME THÉNARDIER: Oh! Mon Dieu! No, sir! She is a little beggar whom we have taken in through charity, a sort of imbecile child. She must have water on the brain; she has a large head, as you see. We do what we can for her, for we are not rich. We have written in vain to her pathetic mother and have received no reply for at least six months. It must be that her mother is dead.

JEAN VALJEAN: Ah.

THÉNARDIER: Her mother didn't amount to much— she abandoned her child.

MADAME THÉNARDIER: Oh! Monsieur, times are so hard! All the people here are poor, you see. If we had not, now and then, some rich and generous travelers like Monsieur, we should not get along at all. We have so many expenses. This child is costing us our very eyes. And then, I have my daughters.

THÉNARDIER: Don't forget we have a son...

MADAME THÉNARDIER: Oh yes, then there's him.

THÉNARDIER: We have no need to bring up other people's children.

JEAN VALJEAN: I see. Well—what do you suppose I take her off your hands for you?

THÉNARDIER: Who?

JEAN VALJEAN: The child.

THÉNARDIER: What child?

JEAN VALJEAN: *(to COSETTE)* Come here, little one.

THÉNARDIER: Ohhh, he wants Collette...

MADAME THÉNARDIER: Cosette, you idiot. *(figuring the bill)* Oh, sir... you already owe us 3 francs for supper, you used a candle—that's 5 francs...

JEAN VALJEAN: I will pay you what I owe you. Tell me what you want for the child.

MADAME THÉNARDIER: Eh! Our little Cosette! Are you intending to take her away from us? Well, I speak frankly: as true as you are an honest man, I will not consent to it. I shall miss her. I saw her first when she was a tiny thing. It is true that she costs us money; it is true that she has her faults; it is true that we are not rich; it is true that I have paid out over four hundred francs for drugs for just one of her illnesses! But one must do something for the good God's sake. She has neither father nor mother. I have brought her up. I have! In truth, I think a great deal of that child. You understand, one conceives an affection for a person. I am a good sort of a beast, I am I do not reason—I love that little girl.

THÉNARDIER: My wife is quick-tempered, but alas, she does love her. You see, she is just the same as our own child.

JEAN VALJEAN: *(mustering some authority)* Is that so? Is that why she is kept in a kennel and works like a dog?

THÉNARDIERS: Well, I... what?

MADAME THÉNARDIER: If I let her go... I must know where you are taking her... I will want to visit my precious...

JEAN VALJEAN: I shall take Cosette away, and that is the end of the matter. You will not know my name, nor our residence. My hope is that we shall never set eyes on you again. I break the thread which binds her foot, and she departs. Does that suit you? Yes or no?

INN MAN 1: Who was this man?

INN PERSON 1: Why this interest?

INN PERSON 2: Why this hideous costume, when he had so much money in his purse?

INN PERSON 3: Could he be Cosette's father? Is he her rich grandfather?

INN PERSON 4: Then why not make himself known at once?

THÉNARDIER: Sir, I am in need of fifteen hundred francs.

> *JEAN VALJEAN takes from his side pocket an old black leather pocketbook, opens it, draws out three bank-bills, and lays them on the table.*

JEAN VALJEAN: Done. Cosette, go and fetch your things.

COSETTE: I don't have any things.

JEAN VALJEAN: Let us go, then. We shall get you some things.

> *COSETTE and JEAN VALJEAN begin to exit.*

MADAME THÉNARDIER: Wait! Is that all? What if I want more??

THÉNARDIER: You are quite right, Me-Lady… Pardon, excuse me, sir, but here are your fifteen hundred francs back. We've changed our minds. We shall take the girl back.

> *COSETTE shudders and presses close to JEAN VALJEAN.*

JEAN VALJEAN: You are going to take back Cosette?

THÉNARDIER: Yes, sir, I am. I will tell you—I have considered the matter… for a brief second. In fact, I have not the right to give her to you. I am an honest man, you see; this child does not belong to me—she belongs to her mother. It was her mother who confided her to me. Yet, if you say to me, "But her mother is dead." In that case, I can only give the child up to the person who shall bring me a writing, signed by her mother, to the effect that I am to hand the child over to the person therein mentioned. Is that clear?

JEAN VALJEAN, without making any reply, fumbles in his pocket. The THÉNARDIERS shiver with joy. He draws out—not bills—but a single paper, and hands it to THÉNARDIER.

JEAN VALJEAN: Read!

THÉNARDIER: *(reading)*
"MONSIEUR THÉNARDIER—
You will deliver Cosette to this person.
He will settle all small debts.
I have the honor of greeting you with kind regards,
FANTINE."

JEAN VALJEAN: You know that signature?

THÉNARDIER: *(recognizing it)* Well, I…

JEAN VALJEAN: You may keep this paper as your receipt.

MADAME THÉNARDIER: Well, you see… we must be paid for all those small debts. A great deal is owed to us.

JEAN VALJEAN: *(standing upright)* Monsieur Thénardier, Madame Thénardier, in January last, the mother reckoned that she owed you one hundred and twenty francs. In February, you sent her a bill of five hundred francs; you received three hundred francs at the end of February, and three hundred francs at the beginning of March. Since then, nine months have

112

elapsed, at fifteen francs a month, the price agreed upon, which makes one hundred and thirty-five francs. You had received one hundred francs too much. That makes you owing me thirty-five francs. Shall we call it even?

THÉNARDIER: Who are you?

JEAN VALJEAN: Come, Cosette.

> *JEAN VALJEAN and COSETTE begin to exit. GUARD 1 and GUARD 2 enter, followed by JAVERT. JEAN VALJEAN escorts COSETTE the other way.*

ÉPONINE: *(watching them exit)* Where are they going?

MADAME THÉNARDIER: Girls, it's time to clean up…

GIRLS: Us!?

AZELMA: Isn't that what the little servant girl is for?

GUARD 2: We are looking for a man…

JAVERT: A man by the name of Jean Valjean.

THÉNARDIER: *(being coy)* How much is it worth to you?

JAVERT: *(grabbing his neck)* I suggest you do not play games with a man who has your life in the palm of his hands.

THÉNARDIER: *(choking)* I don't believe I know him…

JAVERT: *(releases)* Do you have a child here by the name of Cosette?

MADAME THÉNARDIER: Oh, my dear Cosette! She was just taken from us… Will you get her back for us? That terrible man forced us to release her.

JAVERT: Where did they go?

THÉNARDIER: They went out the back.

JAVERT: He will not escape me… I am the law, and he will forever be haunted and pursued.

[INN SCENE FADES TO JEAN VALJEAN AND COSETTE…]

JEAN VALJEAN: Hurry, child. Dear Lord, guide us…

COSETTE: What should I call you?

JEAN VALJEAN: You can call me Papa. Papa Leblanc.

COSETTE: Papa, where are we going?

JEAN VALJEAN: We will make our way to Paris. But we must play a game like hide and seek. Do you know it?

COSETTE: I've watched others play. Are we hiding from Madame Thénardier?

JEAN VALJEAN: That's right… quickly, let's go. I know a man named Father Fauchelevent. He works as a gardener in a convent. We will go there. You will go to school there and become a fine young lady.

COSETTE: Me?

JEAN VALJEAN: Yes. And I will continue to devote my life to our Lord, as the good Bishop has said…

SCENE 4 ~ Luxembourg Gardens, Paris

A lush, parklike setting. PEOPLE pass by, some chatting, some indifferent. GAVROCHE enters through the audience.

GAVROCHE: *(calling out, half song, half defiance)*
Sou for the suffering? Penny for the poor?
No? Then I'll take it, if it feeds the sore!
If pity won't spare me a coin or crust,
I'll feed myself — I must, I must!

TOWNSPERSON: Hey! Stop that boy!

GUARD 1: You little gutter rat! Just wait till I catch you!

GAVROCHE vanishes into the crowd. A group gathers around a makeshift platform. ENJOLRAS and ALICE stand boldly, pamphlets in hand. MARIUS watches from the edge.

ENJOLRAS: People of Paris! Bread has vanished; work is a dream. Must we beg to live in our own city?

ALICE: Is it a crime to be poor? To starve with dignity?

BOTH: No!

ALICE: People, you must be informed. Are you ready to spread the word? Change is needed! The time for change is now! It is time to step out of the darkness of tyranny into the light!

ENJOLRAS: Join us… God forbid that I should diminish France! But embracing Napoleon does not tear her down. Come! Let us argue the question. Where do we stand? Who are we? Who are you? Citizens, my mother is the Republic. We must Revolt.

ALICE: Will you carry the torch with us?

BOTH: Revolt!

Some PASSERBYS nod. Most keep walking. ENJOLRAS and ALICE hand out pamphlets. JAVERT and GUARD 2 observe from nearby.

GUARD 2: Are we just going to let them protest?

JAVERT: I have only just gotten my post here. They have broken no law… yet. But, believe me, if and when they break or bend the law, I will be ready. Perhaps if we go undercover, we will learn of their agenda ahead of time. There is a kind of thrill known to only two creatures on earth — the mother who recovers her child and the tiger who recovers its prey.

GUARD 2: As you say, Inspector.

ALICE hands a pamphlet to a passerby.

ALICE: Here, take one. We meet at the barricade.

ENJOLRAS sees MARIUS approach.

ENJOLRAS: Well, well — Marius! Here to help us distribute truth?

ALICE: Or just chase pretty girls?

MARIUS: I support the cause… but I'm not ready to join the cause.

ENJOLRAS: How are you getting along *without* your family's money?

MARIUS: See these clothes? That's all I've got. I rent a room in a tenement. It's not luxury, but it's mine.

ALICE: I know a watchmaker who'd trade for your pocket watch.

MARIUS: I'm fine. I make enough to get by.

ENJOLRAS: In that case, let's grab a glass… or come to one of our meetings.

MARIUS: I'm waiting for someone.

ENJOLRAS: The girl and her father?

MARIUS: She's like an angel. I call her… Ursula.

ALICE: Ursula?

MARIUS: She left a kerchief. A "U" stitched in gold. What else could I call her?

ENJOLRAS: You're dreaming again. She's out of reach, and now without your inheritance you've nothing to offer.

He hands MARIUS a pamphlet. MARIUS takes it, distractedly. COSETTE and JEAN VALJEAN enter — dignified, finely dressed.

MARIUS: There — do you see her?

ENJOLRAS: You poor, pathetic boy.

MARIUS: *(approaching JEAN VALJEAN)* Good day, Sir… Mademoiselle. Might I offer a pamphlet? Change is stirring in the streets.

JEAN VALJEAN: *(coolly)* No, thank you.

JEAN VALJEAN continues to escort COSETTE, she glances back as they pass.

COSETTE: Papa, wasn't that a bit... cold?

JEAN VALJEAN: The day is pleasant. The gardens are pleasant. The noise — is not.

COSETTE: He seemed... pleasant.

JEAN VALJEAN: He's imprudent at best. Revolutions are for boys with no wives, no wounds. I have known enough chaos. Come.

COSETTE: Perhaps I am a woman now, Papa... with opinions.

JEAN VALJEAN: And opinions get bruised. Let's find another path.

GAVROCHE re-enters. Goes up to JEAN VALJEAN.

GAVROCHE: (*offers hand*) Sir?

JEAN VALJEAN: Small boy, what is the matter with you?

GAVROCHE: The matter is that I am hungry.

JEAN VALJEAN: Here. (*gives bread from COSETTE basket*)

GAVROCHE: *(tartly)* Small boy yourself!

JEAN VALJEAN and COSETTE move on, as does GAVROCHE.

MARIUS: You — boy. Wait.

GAVROCHE: Why do people always say "boy" like it's an insult? Name's Gavroche.

MARIUS: Tell me — do you know that man and his daughter?

GAVROCHE: *(smirks)* Monsieur Leblanc? Maybe. Maybe I watch more than folks think. They help the poor. Hand out bread. But if you want more than crumbs, I take coins.

MARIUS: *(hands a coin)* What else?

GAVROCHE: That's all I know.

MARIUS: *(like he's been had)* Hey?!

GAVROCHE: We're friends! I'll keep an eye out for ya. What's your name? *(starts to move on)*

MARIUS: Marius.

GAVROCHE: Thanks, Marius.

AZELMA and ÉPONINE enter.

MARIUS: Good afternoon. *(to AZELMA and ÉPONINE).*

GAVROCHE begins off. A few note cards fall from GIRLS. They don't notice. MARIUS notices the cards and picks them up and walks on.

AZELMA: Gavroche! If Father sees you—

ÉPONINE: He'll make mincemeat out of you.

AZELMA: *(to ÉPONINE)* I was going to say that!

GAVROCHE: If he feeds me mincemeat first, I'll risk it. It's still a free country… I think?

AZELMA: The garden is our terr...

ÉPONINE: *(watching MARIUS leave)* Who was that? Were you just talking to… Was that our neighbor, Marius?

GAVROCHE: Some fool stuck between love and revolution.

AZELMA: Come, Éponine, we've more letters to hand out. I see that man and girl who gave us bread last week! Maybe I can finagle something out of him today. I am going to work my charm *(fakes cough)* I am!

GAVROCHE: *(mocking their father)* Oh kind sir, a humble father seeks mercy! Spare me. What about his sons? (*He turns to go.*) Run while you can, sisters. The time to get out from Ole Thénadier's clutches is now!

ÉPONINE: I'll meet you at home. I am going to follow a different lead. *(follows MARIUS)*

AZELMA: *(to self)* That's fine, I can do this myself!

Across the way, AZELMA approaches COSETTE and JEAN VALJEAN.

SCENE 5 ~ Apartment House

[MARIUS' APARTMENT...]

ÉPONINE knocks at MARIUS' apartment door.
MARIUS is writing at his desk.

ÉPONINE: Hullo?

MARIUS: What do you wish, Mademoiselle?

ÉPONINE: Here is a letter for you, Monsieur Marius.

MARIUS: You know my name?

ÉPONINE: I live next door. No one tends to notice me, but I'm observant. I have seen you come and go. My father insisted I give this to you.

> *ÉPONINE hands it to him. As MARIUS opens the letter, the seal is still moist. The message could not have come from a distance. While he reads the letter, ÉPONINE looks around the apartment.*

[THÉNADIER'S APARTMENT...]

THÉNADIER: My amiable neighbor, young man: I have learned of your goodness to me, and my family, that you paid my rent six months ago. I bless you, young man. My eldest daughter will tell you that we have been without a morsel of bread for two days, four persons and my spouse ill. I hope that your generous heart will melt at this statement, and you will desire to help us. I am with the distinguished consideration, which is due to the benefactors of humanity, — Jondrette. P.S. My eldest daughter will await your orders, dear Monsieur Marius.

ÉPONINE: You have a mirror! I could look beautiful if I had a mirror.

MARIUS: So, you are part of the family next door.

ÉPONINE: I am Éponine. My apologies for my mum, she can be quite loud.

MARIUS: The walls are paper thin, the plaster broken in places.

ÉPONINE: *(continues to look around)* Ah! books! I know how to read, I do! And I know how to write, too! *(picks up a letter MARIUS was writing).* "When you read this, my soul will be near you and will smile upon you."

MARIUS: Hey, that's private... *(retreats gently)* Mademoiselle, *(ÉPONINE reacts to being called "mademoiselle.")* I must get back to work. But here, I have a package which belongs to you, I think. (*He holds out the envelope containing the four letters he found at the park earlier.*)

ÉPONINE: *(claps her hands)* I have been looking everywhere for that! Dieu de Dieu! It must have been in the park? Sometimes we write phony letters to get money... not like the real one we wrote to you just now. We are starving, you know. We have a Monsieur Leblanc coming tonight to hopefully help us, he felt pity upon my little sister... she reeled him in.

MARIUS: Monsieur Leblanc?

ÉPONINE: Yes. Times are tough... my brothers are already on the streets. What my father says is true. We are starving, and the landlord wants us out... to think my parents used to own an inn... like everyone in France we weren't able to pay the bills and keep it open.

MARIUS: *(feeling empathetic)* Here is money for food. I don't have much myself.

ÉPONINE: There is some sunshine... you are too kind... thank you... Do you know, Mr. Marius, you are a very handsome fellow?

MARIUS: Good day, Éponine.

[THÉNADIER'S APARTMENT...]

MARIUS begins to look through a hole from his apartment.

AZELMA: He is coming!

MADAME THÉNADIER: Who?

AZELMA: The gentleman!

THÉNADIER: The philanthropist?

AZELMA: Yes.

THÉNADIER: From the church of Saint-Jacques?

AZELMA: Yes.

THÉNADIER: That old fellow?

AZELMA: Yes.

MADAME THÉNADIER: And he is coming? You are sure?

AZELMA: I am sure.

Knock at the door

AZELMA: There, truly, he is here. Do I get extra because *I* am the one who he felt pity for?

THÉNADIER: Shh — we will see how generous the old chap is. Quickly, wife — get into bed. Azelma, look sick! Cough already! Now, we can receive the philanthropist. Enter, sir! Deign to enter, most respected benefactor, ohhhh — and your charming young lady, also.

> *JEAN VALJEAN and COSETTE enter. MARIUS, on his perch watching through a crack, recognizes the father and daughter. COSETTE gently lays a package on the table. AZELMA retires behind the door and stares with sombre eyes.*

JEAN VALJEAN: Monsieur, in this package you will find some new clothes and some woolen stockings and blankets.

THÉNADIER: *(bowing deeply, then bending to AZELMA's ear)* Hey? What did I say? Duds! No money! They are all alike! *(aloud)* You bless us dearly.

JEAN VALJEAN: I see that you are greatly to be pitied, Monsieur—

THÉNADIER: You see, my benefactor, no bread, no fire. We are beyond despair. My spouse in bed! Ill!

MADAME THÉNADIER: *(groans)*

COSETTE: Poor woman!

THÉNADIER: And if we do not have the rent… it's to the streets for the Jondrette family. To-morrow is the last day of grace allowed me by my landlord; if by this evening I have not paid my rent, to-morrow my darling daughters, my spouse with her fever,—we shall all four be turned out of here and thrown into the street, on the boulevard, without shelter, in the rain, in the snow. *(abruptly)* I owe sixty francs.

JEAN VALJEAN: Monsieur, these five francs are all that I have about me, but I shall now take my daughter home, and I will return this evening, — I will fetch you the sixty francs.

THÉNADIER: *(aside to MADAME THÉNADIER)* Psst — Take a good look at him, wife!

JEAN VALJEAN: Farewell until this evening, my friends! *(Takes COSETTE's arm, and they turn to go.)*

THÉNADIER: Ta-ta. Farewell. You are a fine gentleman, sir. If only you knew me in better days. We might have been friends. Forgive me, I don't believe I caught your name?

JEAN VALJEAN: Monsieur Lablanc.

THÉNADIER: Did you hear that… Monsieur Lablanc has been sent from heaven. We are saved.

JEAN VALJEAN and COSETTE exit. At that, MARIUS jumps off his spy perch and rushes outside to try to follow JEAN VALJEAN and COSETTE.

[OUTSIDE…]

MARIUS looks both ways... they are gone. While outside, ÉPONINE enters.

ÉPONINE: Good day again, dear sir.

MARIUS: Still you. What do you want with me?

ÉPONINE: My friend, you look sad. What is the matter with you?

MARIUS: I'm sorry, that was rude. There is nothing the matter.

ÉPONINE: Yes, there is! Although you are not rich, you were kind earlier. Be so again now. I do not want you to be grieved. Can I be of any service?

MARIUS: *(confused)* What?

ÉPONINE: Employ me. I do not ask for your secrets, you need not tell them to me, but I may be of use, nevertheless. I may be able to help you. I help my father. When necessary, I carry letters, to go to houses, find out addresses…

MARIUS: An address! Yes… your sister brought hither that old gentleman and his daughter! Do you know them? Do you know their address?

ÉPONINE: No.

MARIUS: Find it for me. Can you do it?

ÉPONINE: Will that make you happy?

MARIUS: Oh, very much so! *(grabs her hand)*

ÉPONINE: (looks down at their hands) Consider it yours. (ÉPONINE runs off)

MADAME THÉNADIER: You've got a twinkle in your eye… you are coming up with a plan, aren't you?

THÉNADIER: *(picks up a walking stick)* He won't know what hit him.

MADAME THÉNADIER: You are sure it's him?

THÉNADIER: I'm telling you that I am sure of it, I recognize him. Sure! Eight years have passed! But I recognize him! Ah! I recognize him. Why—didn't you?

MADAME THÉNADIER: No. But I was stuck in bed, ill, remember?

THÉNADIER: But I told you: 'Pay attention!' Why… it is his figure, it is his face, only older, —there are people who do not grow old, I don't know how they manage it, —nevertheless it was the very sound of his voice! He is better dressed, that is all! Ah! You mysterious old devil, I've got you, that I have!

MADAME THÉNADIER: When I think that my daughters are going barefoot and have not a gown to their backs! What! That horrible, beautiful young lady, who gazed at my Azelma with an air of pity, —she is that beggar brat! Oh! I should like to kick her in her stomach!

THÉNADIER: Azelma, go get that blasted sister of yours. We must also gather our pathetic posse of poor unfortunate souls. We are about to cash in!

AZELMA exits.

THÉNADIER: Do you know, it's mighty lucky, that the idiot didn't recognize me! If he had, he would not have come back again. He would have slipped through our fingers! It was my beard that saved us! My romantic beard! My pretty little romantic beard! And I have a plan for him, I do.

[OUTSIDE. LIGHTS on MARIUS back at street, talking to some REVOLUTIONISTS...]

REVOLUTIONISTS exit.

AZELMA: Excuse me, have you seen my sister? I need to find her promptly...

MARIUS: Oh? She went on an errand I believe.

AZELMA: *(whispers, brings him in)* Can you keep a secret? My Father is conjuring up a plan... Sounds like Monsieur Lablanc is about to be la-broke.

MARIUS: Oh!? What about the girl?

AZELMA: Ma-ma says we shall have all her pretty things... she's likely to become a gutter rat herself. Now where is my sister? Monsieur Lablanc will be back soon. I better find her... and I need to get my father's band of ruffians, they will want a piece of him as well. *(sets off)*

MARIUS: I must report this... *(exits)*

[THÉNADIER APARTMENT...]

MARIUS enters with JAVERT and GUARDS.
MARIUS is explaining what he knows. Meanwhile

JEAN VALJEAN is in the room with the THÉNADIERS.

MADAME THÉNADIER: We're so glad you came back.

THÉNADIER: You do not know me? Well, I know you! I knew you immediately. You are going to find out at last it is not all roses to go into people's houses *or inns* under false pretexts. Pay up, Monsieur Madeleine! We'll take everything you got now… including the spoiled brat.

MADAME THÉNADIER: My precious daughters could use a house maid again…

JEAN VALJEAN: *(calmly)* You will not lay a hand on my daughter.

THÉNADIER: *(begins to lunge and struggle begins)* I will gnaw your heart tonight. You will pay handsomely…

    SFX: *Whistle. JAVERT begins to move forward.*

AZELMA: (*Enters*) Pa-Pa, it's police!!

    JEAN VALJEAN and THÉNADIER struggle. JEAN VALJEAN gets away.

JAVERT: Open up. (*JAVERT and SOLDIERS enter*)

THÉNADIER: We were being robbed. The thief got away.

JAVERT: Your "gang of thugs" told us your plan… Someone should have told your victim generosity doesn't pay.

AZELMA: Ma-ma. Please, sir! I don't know them. They've taken me hostage. I don't want to go to jail.

MADAME THÉNADIER: Be quiet, child! This is all your fault. You brought him here.

JAVERT: Up to your old tricks again, eh Jondrette. When will you learn? Take them all in…

THÉNADIER: We are innocent. You can't prove anything. It was self-defense.

JAVERT: The law will always catch up with people like you. I am the law, and the law will not be mocked. I rid the streets of vermin like you.

> *GUARDS escort THÉNADIERS out. GUARD 3 enters.*

GUARD 3: Inspector Javert, we just got word… General Lamarque has died. The rebels are increasing their numbers… the mourning may turn into revolt.

JAVERT: Perhaps I will join them…

GUARD 3: The rebels, sir?

JAVERT: Just a little plan… It's time to go retrieve my disguise.

SCENE 6 ~ Luxembourg Gardens

*MARIUS enters. MEMBERS OF THE ABC are
rallying, including ALICE and GAVROCHE.*

ENJOLRAS: Marius, my friend! Tomorrow, we meet at
the barricade. Will you be there?

MARIUS: I… I still don't know.

ENJOLRAS: You better decide soon. The revolution
will wait for no one.

GAVROCHE: Come on. We're going to pitch the
government!

MARIUS: Oh, I see, recruiting them young (and
perhaps a bit small) there, Enjolras!

GAVROCHE: Little folks are good for something!! I
can fight! Who says I can't?

MARIUS: I don't doubt you.

GAVROCHE: That's right! Trust the little folks,
distrust the big!

ALICE: Come on, you two we have more pamphlets to
hand out.

ENJOLRAS: I hope we see you tonight, Marius!

ÉPONINE enters.

ÉPONINE: It's you… Marius! I have been looking for
you! You don't seem glad to see me?

MARIUS: Éponine, did you learn anything?

ÉPONINE: You know my name? Barricades are going up. But I suppose you want to know the address of a certain someone.

MARIUS: Did you find Ursula?

ÉPONINE: Oh—you wanted to find the girl… Her name is *Cosette*. I don't see what is so special about her…

MARIUS: *(utters "Cosette" quietly)* Do you know where she lives? I must see her…

ÉPONINE: Here. *(holds out a piece of paper)*

MARIUS: Oh, Éponine. You sweet, wonderful woman! *(spins her, and runs off)*

> *ÉPONINE stands in awe for a second. GAVROCHE comes back to her, jabs her with a pamphlet and they BOTH go off together. JAVERT comes in with disguise, also gets a pamphlet and is welcomed in by ALICE.*

GENDARME 1: Inspector, is that their leader?

JAVERT: Stop calling me inspector! We are spies. Our job is not to comment on the situation, merely to report on revolutionary activity. You know your orders—your job will be to find out where these anarchists, the Friends of the ABC, meet. Integrate yourself into their company, find out their plans and report back to headquarters. I want to know their names, where they live, what type of wine they drink—everything they do. Am I understood?

GENDARME 1: Yes, sir.

JAVERT: You there, *(to ENJOLRAS)* how does one enlist…?

ENJOLRAS: Welcome, my good sir! Right this way…

SCENE 7 ~ Outside Lablanc Residence

COSETTE is strolling outside. JEAN VALJEAN enters.

JEAN VALJEAN: Cosette, what are you doing outside? I told you to stay indoors.

COSETTE: It was such a beautiful evening, I wanted to try to look for stars. *(notices JEAN VALJEAN is hurt)* Papa, what is it? What did you do?

JEAN VALJEAN: It's nothing. I'll be fine. But we must leave here. The city is not safe. You need to pack your things.

COSETTE: What if I want to stay!?

JEAN VALJEAN: You want to stay for that young gentleman you seek?

COSETTE: You keep me locked up tight, as if I were in a prison.

JEAN VALJEAN: Don't talk to me about prison…

COSETTE: How could I when you don't confide in me? I feel as if I do not know anything about you! What are you hiding? Where are we going now? Why do you keep locked drawers and packed bags? I do not even know my mother's name! Is it fear, is it shame? Tell me—something!

JEAN VALJEAN: We will leave in two days. Be ready. *(exits)*

COSETTE begins to cry. MARIUS enters.

MARIUS: There, there. You are far too beautiful to cry. What makes you so sad?

COSETTE: Fine sir, it is you.

MARIUS: Do not be afraid of me. You are my angel.

COSETTE: Here we are… together.

MARIUS: Together, at last. I have watched you for so many months. I feel like I have watched you blossom…

COSETTE: I am about to wilt. My father is taking me away. We are going away.

MARIUS: What? But I finally found you…

COSETTE: Will you follow? God should not wish to separate us?

MARIUS: I have no money. But without you I am nothing. Here. *(hands her a love note)*

COSETTE: I don't even know your name. *(begins to cry again)*

MARIUS: Oh, my dear Cosette— *(surprised he knows her name)* you will always be in my heart. And I will forever be your Marius, even if we can't be together. I will go and fight for the cause. Perhaps I will become some sort of hero worthy of your hand. *(exits)*

JEAN VALJEAN enters again.

JEAN VALJEAN: You are still out here.

COSETTE: Oh, Papa. He's gone… (hands him the note/poem; they embrace).

JEAN VALJEAN: I see. Go inside. We will make some tea and we will talk… *(speaks to God)* God, on high. I tried to lock her up and protect her. What I do at this moment you behold from on high, and that is sufficient. You say, if we love each other, you live in us and your love is brought to full expression in us. Thank you, from the depths of my soul, that you have permitted me, a miserable man, that I should be loved by this innocent being. I will go, I will find this young man and return him home.

SCENE 8 ~ Barricade

Drum roll sounds. A barricade is up.
REVOLUTIONISTS around. JAVERT included.

ENJOLRAS: Listen, these are our streets! They belong to everybody.

REVOLUTIONISTS: Cheer!

ENJOLRAS: This is our country! Vive la Republique!

MARIUS enters... followed shortly after by JEAN VALJEAN...

REVOLUTIONISTS: Vive la Republique!

ENJOLRAS: *(to self)* Strange how the sky turns blue, when the world turns red. *(aloud)* This barricade is made neither of paving stones, nor of timbers, nor of iron; it is made of a mound of ideas and a mound of sorrows. Here misery encounters the ideal. Here the day embraces the night and says: I will die with you and you will be born again with me. *Vive la Republique!*

ALL: Vive la Republique!

ENJOLRAS: Marius! I always knew you would come!

ALICE: Fortify that barricade! They are getting closer!

GAVROCHE: Reporting for duty, monsieur.

MARIUS: Gavroche? What are you doing here?

GAVROCHE: I want the big musket!

ENJOLRAS: Tell me what have you seen? *(to MARIUS)* Gavroche is an excellent informant.

GAVROCHE: The barricade is blocked in. They are starting to advance. See — little folks are good for something! Don't ye remember, trust the little folks, distrust the big — in fact, you *(pulls MARIUS and ENJOLRAS closer)* see that big fellow there? *(JAVERT)* He is a spy.

MARIUS: Are you sure?

GAVROCHE: Yeah. Remember you told me to keep an eye out on your lady friend, right? Well, he's been nosing about her home as well — in uniform. He's an Inspector.

MARIUS: Well done my little street rat.

> *MARIUS and MEN advance toward JAVERT, who is loading a pistol.*

ENJOLRAS: You, there! Who are you? *(MEN grab JAVERT)*

JAVERT: My name is Javert.

MARIUS: Are you a revolutionary, Javert? Where are your papers?

JAVERT: No need, I am who the urchin says I am… I am Inspector Javert.

GAVROCHE: The mouse has caught the cat. I has.

JAVERT: You are all miserable creatures! You will never defeat the law. Do what you must with me… your efforts today will be futile.

ENJOLRAS: Tie him up… we have no time for him.

ALICE: He must be executed!

JEAN VALJEAN: *(steps up)* Allow me. I am here to help.

MARIUS: I know this man. We can trust him.

JEAN VALJEAN takes JAVERT aside.

ENJOLRAS: Permission granted. Now come on. It has come, my friends — the day when all shall be concord, harmony, light, joy, and life. It will come — and it is for that day that we are going to die. Do you hear the silence before the storm? It listens for our names. We are not men of power, but of principle. We carry no crowns — only courage. Let others build palaces — we build hope with broken furniture and unbroken hearts. This barricade is not wood and stone — it is made of fire and dream. And though they may crush us, they will never unwrite what we stood for. They will say we were fools, or children, or lost — Let them. History does not remember those who wait. We are not waiting. We are becoming the dawn.

More fighting.

ALICE: A quarter of an hour more and we won't have any cartridges left!

GAVROCHE: Then it's to the streets I go… I'm a pickpocket… I'll get us what we need. There's plenty of full cartridges on the dead.

ALICE: Gavroche! Gavroche! *(she gets shot)*

GAVROCHE: I'm small and I'm quick… Besides, they won't fire at me, I'm too quick for that.

*GAVROCHE climbs over the barricade and starts looting a few dead bodies littering the stage. **SFX**: Rifle shots. Dead bodies twitch as if being shot.*

MARIUS: Get back here! They're firing on you! Come back, you little, stupid boy!

GAVROCHE gets shot.

ENJOLRAS: Remember my friends we are fighting for France! Attack! We won't give up without a fight! For Gavroche!

MARIUS and ENJOLRAS shot.

[SCENE SHIFTS TO JAVERT AND JEAN VALJEAN...]

JAVERT: It's you... you can finally take your revenge on me, Jean Valjean!

They stare at each other for a moment, rage on both their faces. JEAN VALJEAN uncocks the pistol and shoves it in his belt. He then takes a knife out of his pocket and opens it.

JAVERT: Ah — a knife! You're right, that suits you better. *(JEAN VALJEAN cuts him free.)*

JEAN VALJEAN: You are free.

JAVERT: Who are you? I have hunted you my entire life. And it ends here. Kill me.

JEAN VALJEAN: I am not who you think I am. I am no longer the man who stole a loaf of bread to feed my sister's family. I am not the man who took silver from the only man on earth at the time to love me. I am not the man who robbed a little boy of his forty precious sou. I am Jean Valjean. Go on. I said you are free.

JAVERT: Who are you to give me life? I am the law! I get the last say! *(JAVERT takes out a hidden gun, points it at JEAN VALJEAN... but can't)*

JEAN VALJEAN: It's called mercy. Now go. This story is over...

> *A gun shot is heard. JEAN VALJEAN returns to the fighting.*

[BARRICADE...]

REVOLUTIONIST: *(bloodied)* The street's blocked. The alley — go through the alley!

> *JEAN VALJEAN goes to MARIUS... checks on him...*

JEAN VALJEAN: *(kneeling beside MARIUS)* Marius... Marius, keep fighting! Let's bring you home.

REVOLUTIONIST: *(bloodied)* Let's go!

JEAN VALJEAN: *(lifts MARIUS carefully)* I will not leave you.

REVOLUTIONIST: *(choked)* We all leave something here. Leave with what we can.

JEAN VALJEAN: *(to MARIUS, softly)* You have someone waiting. I'll carry you home.

> *JEAN VALJEAN lifts MARIUS on his shoulders. A hush falls over the barricade. Distant commands echo as soldiers prepare to charge. Smoke thickens.*

141

JEAN VALJEAN: *(low, to himself)* Through sewer or fire, by grace or grave — I will carry you home.

JEAN VALJEAN disappears into the smoke as the sound of the enemy's march rises. The flag at the barricade flutters once and falls.

SCENE 9 ~ Home

JEAN VALJEAN lies on a bed, still and pale. The audience may assume it is MARIUS at first. DOCTOR/BISHOP tends to him. COSETTE is nearby, anxious.

COSETTE: Doctor, is he going to pull through? I can't lose him. Please tell me he shall live.

DOCTOR/BISHOP: He has suffered greatly. I believe he begins his walk, that his soul may be reconciled with God, in whom he trusts.

COSETTE: No, no! Papa! You shall live.

JEAN VALJEAN stirs.

JEAN VALJEAN: Cosette? You forbid me to die? Oh, Cosette, it is nothing to die; it is frightful not to live.

MARIUS enters, walking with a cane, a bandage around his head.

COSETTE: I have called for a priest.

JEAN VALJEAN: *(looking to Heavenly Father)* That's alright. I have one. *(to MARIUS)* Marius, you live.

MARIUS: I hear you are to thank.

COSETTE: Thank you, Papa.

JEAN VALJEAN: Come closer, the both of you. My name is Jean Valjean. I love you dearly. I do not wish you to have any deep grief. I am not going very far. You will only have to look up when it's night. *(FANTINE enters in white)* You will see me, and Cosette, your

143

mother there. Her name is Fantine. She suffered much, but like our Father, she loves you always. Love each other dearly always. There is scarcely anything else in the world but that: to love one another.

JEAN VALJEAN exhales and dies.

COSETTE: No, Papa!

DOCTOR/BISHOP: He is gone. He wanted you two to have these candlesticks. He said, although they are silver… they are priceless to him. Keep being light in the darkness.

FADE TO BLACK

PRONUNCIATION GUIDE

Characters

Name	Pronunciation
Jean Valjean	ZHAHN val-ZHAHN
Javert	zhah-VEHR
Fantine	fahn-TEEN
Cosette	koh-ZETT
Marius Pontmercy	MAH-ree-us pon-mehr-SEE
Éponine	ay-poh-NEEN
Gavroche	gah-VROSH
Madame Thénardier	mah-DAHM tay-nar-DYAY
Monsieur Thénardier	muh-SYUH tay-nar-DYAY
Enjolras	ahn-zhohl-RAHS
Grantaire	grahn-TEHR
Combeferre	kohm-fehr
Courfeyrac	koor-feh-RAK

Towns & Places

Place	Pronunciation
Digne	DEEN-yeuh
Montreuil-sur-Mer	mohn-TREU-yee sir mehr
Paris	pah-REE
Arras	ah-RAHS
Vernon	vehr-NAWN
Montfermeil	mohn-fehr-MAY

Supporting Characters & Mentions

Name	Pronunciation
Monseigneur Bienvenu	mohn-seh-NYUR byan-vuh-NEW
Fauchelevent	FOHSH-luh-VAHN
Champmathieu	shahn-mah-TYUH
Petit Gervais	puh-TEE zher-VEH
Montparnasse	mohn-par-NASS
Brevet	bruh-VEH
Cochepaille	KAWSH-pah-yuh
Chenildieu	shuh-NEEL-dyuh
Bamatabois	bah-mah-tah-BWAH
Blachevelle	blash-eh-VELL
Listolier	lees-toh-lee-AY
Fameuil	fah-MUH-yuh

GLOSSARY

Term	Meaning	Pronunciation
Sou	1/20 of a franc (small coin)	soo
Franc	French currency unit	frahnk
Gendarme	Armed police officer	zhahn-DARM
Savoyard	Street child from Savoy	sah-vwah-YAR
Misérables	The wretched, the poor	mee-zay-RAHB-luh (Fr.) / miz-uh-RAH-buhlz (Eng.)

ACKNOWLEDGEMENTS

This project would not have been possible without the love, encouragement, and support of so many. First and foremost, I give thanks to my Lord and Savior, Jesus Christ—the true Light in the darkness. Without His grace and guidance, none of this story, nor any light within it, could exist.

To my husband, Jim—thank you for being my steadfast lighthouse, guiding me through both calm waters and stormy seas, even in the wee morning hours of writing.

To my students—thank you for boldly stepping into the shoes of these characters, bringing them to life, and reminding us all that stories shine brightest when shared from the heart. To my faithful test readers—Kristi, Kelly, Kristen, Josiah, Melissa, Amber, and Ellen—your words were lanterns along my path, casting light where it was needed most. To my family—thank you for your unwavering love and encouragement. And to my Valley Troubadour sisters in Christ—Cathy, Schawn, and Carolyn—it has been an honor to walk alongside you, creating productions that illuminate hearts and point to Him.

Each of you, and so many more, including Victor Hugo, has been a vital spark in the making of Light in the Darkness. Together, you've reminded me that even the smallest flame can cast away shadows, and that on every stage, His light shines brightest of all.

Light in the Darkness, a stage adaptation Inspired by Victor Hugo's *Les Misérables*, received its premiere production by the Troubadours Players in Appleton, Wisconsin, on November 6, 2025. The original cast was as follows:

Name	Character
Ally Schoessow	Fantine
Annalee Ernst	M. Thénardier
Annika Quinones	Alice / Townsperson 1
Benjamin Leavins	Jacquin
Benjamin Neumann	Javert
Blake Rosenau	Jean Valjean
Cecily Schleicher	M. Victurnien
Charlotte Bell	Azelma
Claire Fochs	Child / Bystander
Corbin Buettner	Father Fauchelevent
Corbin Heitz	Cochepaille / Husband
Elizabeth Lindsay	Nun / Inn Guest
Ellie Lovett	Worker 2
Emma Kulus	Worker 1
Faith Tower	M. Baptistine / Margueritte
Forrest Boocher	Prosecutor
Frances Kosmicki	Worker 3
Gloria Strasburg	Cosette
Hailey Janssen	Wife
Hannah Janssen	Worker 4
Hope Malueg	Townsperson 7

Irene Guevara	Marquise de R
Janessa Warrick	Éponine
Jocelyn Spencer	Dahlia
Johanna Vandenberg	M. Magloire/Townsperson 4
Joshua Schmitz	Gavroche
Josiah Humbert	Guard
Joy Tower	Landlady
Lilliana Rex	Sister Simplicity
Luke LaFrombois	Thénardier
Natalie Humbert	Townsperson 2 / Favourite
Noah Dufek	Enjolras/Felix
Noah Rex	Brevet/Guard
Noah Thiel	Bamatabois / Champmathieu
Reagan Johnson	Inn Guest
Sam Caravella	Bishop
Samantha Voss	Zéphine / Quack Dentist
Sharlette Hasse	Gervais
Titus Nelsen	Marius

ABOUT THE AUTHOR

Heather Neumann is a passionate director and playwright. She has written numerous adaptations, bringing both classic tales and fresh narratives to life. Heather finds deep joy in working with young performers, helping them discover their voice and the power it carries to impact the world. With a gift for transforming timeless literature into accessible and compelling dramas for high school students, Heather's work is infused with purpose, beauty, and grace. Her greatest delight is in revealing the love of the Father through every performance. She treasures her faith, her family, and the way theater can draw hearts closer to Jesus.